A GLOSSARY OF MORPHOLOGY

A Glossary
of Morphology

Laurie Bauer

Georgetown University Press
Washington, D.C.

© Laurie Bauer, 2004

Georgetown University Press
Washington, D.C.

10 9 8 7 6 5 4 3 2 1   2004

This book is printed on acid-free paper meeting the requirements of the
American National Standard for Permanence in Paper for Printed Library
Materials.

First published in the United Kingdom by
Edinburgh University Press.

Library of Congress Cataloging-in-Publication Data

Bauer, Laurie, 1949–
     A glossary of morphology / Laurie Bauer.
          p. cm.
Includes bibliographical references.
     ISBN 1-58901-043-4 (pbk. : alk. paper)
   1. Grammar, Comparative and general—Morphology–Terminology. I. Title.
     P241.B378 2004
     415′.9′014–dc22

                              2004013172

Typeset in Sabon
by Norman Tilley Graphics, Northampton, and
printed and bound in Finland.

Contents

Preface

A glossary is a strange kind of book, by nature one that is dipped into rather than one which is read from cover to cover, so that the reader rather than the author controls the order in which the various sections are met. It therefore requires certain rules if readers are to find their way around in it.

Cross-references to other entries in the glossary are provided in **bold** type. Sometimes this cross-reference has to be interpreted rather loosely: the bold item **derivational** may actually refer to an entry headed **derivation**. However, not all words which are entries in the glossary are in bold type everywhere they occur. Rather, bold type indicates that useful information is likely to be found in the cross-reference. Single quotation marks enclose alternative technical terms and other technical terms referred to. At the same time, it must be recalled that only terms relating to morphology have a place in this glossary: terms relating to phonology, syntax or semantics may be used, even explained, but they are not part of the glossary.

Some writers on morphology have been given privileged position by having their work referred to in the glossary without a full reference. The works referred to in these cryptic references are listed in the Fundamental Works at the end of the book. There is also a fuller bibliography of suggested further reading. At the end of the book there are also two indexes: an index of names and an index of languages, to help the reader find references to individual scholars or particular examples.

While a glossary like this is a dictionary of a kind, it is also a linguistics book, and adheres to certain conventions of linguistics books. Among these is the convention that examples presented as part of the text are italicised. '*Cars* remained unusual' means that the word *cars* remained unusual, not that automobiles remained unusual. Also, single quotation marks are used to contain glosses, for example: French *aimer* 'to love'.

As well as being a linguistics book, this is a morphology book, and there are notational conventions associated with morphology which are also adhered to, including the use of small capitals to indicate lexemes. See the entry for **notational conventions**.

Not only is a glossary a hard book to read, it is a hard book to write. As in all lexicography, details are important, and getting them consistently right is, as linguists might say, a non-trivial exercise. I have been very greatly helped by Andrew Carstairs-McCarthy and Winifred Bauer, who have pointed out errors of omission and commission in an earlier draft. Thanks also to Mark Aronoff. Those errors that remain can all be blamed on me.

Wellington, January 2004

Introduction

As a branch of linguistics, morphology deals with the structure of words. This simple definition requires a little explanation though, since words have several types of structure. It can be rephrased as follows. Morphology deals with the correlation of form and meaning within the word. An example should make this clearer.

Consider the set of words illustrated in (1) below.

(1) Some related words in English

COLUMN 1	COLUMN 2	COLUMN 3
beggar	beggarly	beggarliness
friend	friendly	friendliness
lord	lordly	lordliness
man	manly	manliness
mother	motherly	motherliness
neighbour	neighbourly	neighbourliness
woman	womanly	womanliness

The word in Column 2 always indicates an adjective meaning 'like or suitable for the person mentioned in Column 1'. So *neighbourly* means 'like or suitable for a neighbour' and so on. These meanings are associated with a constant difference in form: there is always an extra *-ly* (or we could formulate the same thing in terms of sounds) at the end of the word. The difference in meaning between the words in Columns 2 and 3 is likewise predictable on the basis of their form. The word in Column 3 always means 'a characteristic of people who can be described by the word in Column 2' (so that *motherliness* means 'a characteristic of motherly people'). Again the difference in form is the same in all the Column 3 words, the addition of *-ness* and, in the spelling though not in the sounds, a change from *y* to *i* immediately before the *-ness*. These examples show a correlation between form (e.g. the addition of *-ness*) and meaning (e.g. the addition of the meaning 'a characteristic of being like a person'). These are morphological relationships, the kind of patterns that morphology accounts for.

The words in Column 1 are also related in meaning. They all mean 'person' of some kind. This semantic relationship is, however, not reflected in any shared form among the words in this column. It is true that *man* and *woman* both have the letters *man* in them, but the letters are pronounced differently in the two cases, and the common sound at the end of *beggar* and *mother* is spelled differently – and in any case it appears to be accidental. These words may share semantic features, but they do not share morphological structure.

Now consider some further words which end in the same letters or sounds as those in Column 2. These will help to refine the notion of what counts as a morphological relationship. The words *assembly*, *belly*, *early*, *hopefully*, *lily*, *silly* all have a relationship in form with the words in Column 2, but there is no meaning in common. These words share some phonological (or orthographic) structure, but do not share a morphological structure.

Bearing in mind the fact that likeness in structure should be meaningful likeness and not random likeness, we can say that morphology as a discipline within linguistics is concerned with the relationship of form and meaning within the word. One task that morphologists undertake is to describe the patterns like those in (1) which are found in individual languages, and state the rules by which words may be constructed morphologically in each language. The words in (1) show one type of (rather trivial) rule in application: to add -*ness* to a word which ends in -*ly*, change the *y* to an *i* in the spelling. But further examples show rules on other levels as well. For example, Column 1 can be extended by adding words in like *gentleman, matron, priest, scholar* and so on, but the pattern apparently does not apply to *child* and *lady*. Is there something about these two words which excludes them from Column 1, and if so what might it be? Or is it possible but unusual to add these words to Column 1?

There are further questions about the patterns in (1). In (1) all the bits of extra material were added at the end of the original words. Is this a general rule about languages? Patterns like those in (2) show that the rule is not always true, at least in English. Yet it turns out that more languages put material after the original word than before it, and most languages prefer the kind of structure in (1) to the kind of structure in (2).

(2) Another set of related English words

COLUMN 1	COLUMN 2	COLUMN 3
body	embody	disembody
power	empower	disempower
slave	enslave	disenslave
tangle	entangle	disentangle

Column 2 in (2) raises another point. Why do some words have *em-* and some *en-* in front of the original word? Although so few examples have been given in (2), a little thought and perhaps some time consulting a dictionary will provide a reason. The form *em-* is used before words which start with the letters *b* or *p*. Why should *em-* occur in precisely those places? It is not really to do with the spelling, but to do with the sounds which that spelling represents. The sounds /b/ and /p/ are produced with both lips, as is /m/ but not /n/. We find /m/ before sounds produced with both lips, and *en-* elsewhere. This implies that a word beginning with *m* would also have *em-*. There are very few words of English where the hypothesis could be tested, but one dictionary lists *emmarble* (though not *disemmarble*). This leads into a different set of questions. Is *en-* an element in the word-structure of English? If so, it would be necessary to say that this element has two variants, *em-* and *en-*, and that the two of them divide up the set of words they can attach to between them. Linguists call this situation 'complementary distribution', and take it as a centrally important principle in determining when two distinct elements (like *em-* and *en-*) should count as the same for some other purpose.

In the discussion above, all the specific terms for elements or their relationships have been avoided. The glossary focuses on these technical terms. While it would no doubt be possible to learn about morphology by reading the glossary through thoroughly and noting all the links from one term to another, it is assumed that the reader's fundamental introduction to morphology will come from some discussion which uses the various terms – perhaps the discussion in a textbook (of which there are several listed in the bibliographical material at the end of the book) or the description of a particular language.

However, a word of caution is needed: not all authors use the same words to mean (fundamentally) the same thing, and not all authors use the same term in precisely the same way. Sometimes different terms are used because the old one has gone out of fashion – possibly because its implications were felt to be inaccurate, possibly because a term from a different theory of word-structure has become the normal term. Terms are not always used in precisely the same way because linguists adapt the terms to their own theories, and the implications may not be the same in other theories. The people using the terms may or may not realise that they are extending or restricting the use, or they may do it deliberately because of the constraints of the theory they are working with. It is unfortunate that the two least consistently used terms of morphology are the fundamental terms of morphological study: *word* and *morpheme*. They thus require special explanation in the glossary. Other terms arise in the context of particular theories, or are invented by particular scholars and become general. While the names of the first people to use terms have not been consistently given, they are given from time to time in the glossary, and where terms are used predominantly within certain theories, this is also noted.

To some extent, the theories are tied to the period at which the discussion of word-structure is carried out and the country in which it was carried out. In the classical tradition the main part of morphology was the part which lists the different forms of words. Until well through the twentieth century, young scholars of Latin were taught to recite the forms in which pattern nouns or verbs could occur in much the same way that they recited their times tables at the same period and for much the same reason: just as you could not do arithmetic without knowing the answers to particular multiplications automatically, so you could not produce or understand Latin properly without knowing automatically which form of each noun or verb meant precisely what.

In the structuralist era, the focus shifted from the words to the elements within the words. The term *morpheme* was coined, apparently by the Polish scholar Jan Baudouin de Courtenay in the late nineteenth century. This term was taken up on both sides of the Atlantic, though interpreted slightly differently in different places and at different times. It also served as the foundation for a host of other names of elements of words. Many of those terms are explained in this book.

In more recent times, morphology has been built into the various linguistic theories in circulation, sometimes being seen as fundamentally a part of syntax and sharing many syntactic features, sometimes being seen as fundamentally a part of phonology and being discussed in phonological terms, sometimes being seen as bridging syntax and phonology, and sometimes being viewed as an independent part of grammatical structure. Sometimes morphological facts are seen as things to be taken into account by a grammatical model, sometimes the aim has been to explain them in terms of wider cognitive abilities. In every case, the treatments of morphological phenomena leave behind them a trace in the form of some terminology, some of it mainly restricted to use within a particular theory, some of it becoming much more generally used in the morphological community. In a book this size it is not possible to list all these terms, but an attempt has been made to list those which are widely recognised.

Early in the Classical tradition of Graeco-Roman grammatical studies, lists of the possible morphological structures of words constituted the main part of any grammar. It is not until well after the height of the Roman empire that syntax came to play an important part in grammatical description. Even then, syntax started out as the study of how to use words with particular morphological structures. Today, when syntax is given pride of place as the central topic in linguistic structure, mediating between the unpredictable forms listed in the lexicon and the semantic interpretation of propositions, the Classical view strikes us as quaint. Yet morphology can still be seen as playing a central part in linguistic study.

First, although care has been taken to show that morphological structure and phonological structure are distinct, the one can influence the other. In some places stress patterns are associated with morphological structures: consider the difference in stress between *pro'ductiveness* and *produc'tivity*, which depends on precisely which morphological elements are used). In other places sequences of consonants and vowels are affected: if -y is added to *secret*, the result is *secrecy* with a *c* or phonologically with an /s/ rather than **secrety*; if -y is added to *fidget* the result is *fidgety*. So morphology cannot be isolated from phonology.

It is also closely related to syntax: morphological elements are used to show how words function in sentences. In a Latin sentence such as *Agricola puellam vidit* 'the farmer saw the girl', the final -*m* on *puellam* shows that it is the girl who is seen, not who did the seeing. *Agricolam puella vidit* means 'the girl saw the farmer'. Syntactic structure and morphological structure are in some way intertwined: one of them dictates forms used in the other.

Morphology is also closely associated with our vocabulary or lexicon. We use morphological principles to create new words like *institutionalisation* (a technical term of morphology). Morphological patterns structure our vocabulary and make it manageable for us, revealing the parallels between words like *centralisation*, *formalisation*, *industrialisation*, *normalisation* and so on.

Morphology is sometimes related to our spelling system. While many people are unsure how to spell *grammar*, the second *a* is clearly heard in *grammarian*. The *g* that is not pronounced in *sign* is heard in *signal* and *signify*. The silent *n* in *autumn* is pronounced in the word *autumnal*.

Morphological links often contribute to the coherence of a text. Woodrow Wilson, in a speech in 1919, said,

> Some people call me an idealist. Well that is the way I know I am an American. America, my fellow citizens, ... America is the only idealistic nation in the world.

The word *idealistic* picks up and refers back to the earlier *idealist*, even though it occurs in a different syntactic environment. In fact, it could be argued that one of the functions of morphological constructions is to allow us to put 'the same word' into different syntactic environments.

Morphology has contributed a lot to the field of psycholinguistics. There has been a great deal of argument in recent years about the way in which our brains cope with the fact that we have regular verbs like *walk*, which has past-tense form *walked*, and irregular verbs like *run* and *go*, which have unpredictable past-tense forms *ran* and *went* respectively. The answers to these disputes will no doubt help us understand the way language is processed more generally in the brain.

While morphology has not been discussed much within sociolinguistics, there are clear instances where differences in morphological constructions are linked to social or regional differences. Some morphological patterns are used more in one geographical region than in another (a word like *shootee* 'a person who is shot' is more likely to arise in American than in British English), or in certain social domains (a word like *sockie* 'little sock' is more likely to arise in language used by or to children than among adults), or by people of different ages (*dove* is more likely to be used as the past tense of *dive* by young speakers of English than by older ones). Some morphological patterns are restricted to fairly formal language, while others are informal by nature. All the social influences which affect other aspects of language can be seen to influence morphology as well.

Morphology has certainly been extensively studied in historical linguistics (particularly with relation to analogical change) and in linguistic typology (for example, in relation to whether heads or dependants of heads take morphological marking).

We can see that morphology stands at what one writer has called a 'crossroads' for many different aspects of linguistic study, as well as in a position where it is of value to many different approaches to linguistics. Its importance as a field of study cannot be in doubt.

This book is an alphabetic guide to morphological terminology. It can be used as a dictionary. It can also be read thematically, moving from article to related article to see how various aspects of morphological study are treated together as packages which we call morphological theories. The theories are mentioned here, but the particular elements which they pack together are not given great weight. Rather, if you read thematically you will discover that where there are two possible ways of viewing a particular morphological phenomenon, certain other beliefs or answers to problems tend to be associated with one and not with the other view. Morphology is a developing science. In less than a hundred years it has moved from being seen as central to linguistics but rather boring (because predictable), to being seen as something which exists round the borders of what linguists are interested in, to being back in the centre because what happens in morphology has implications for so much else. Being the centre of theoretical attention does not make morphology the easiest field of linguistics to deal with at the moment, but it makes sure that it stays interesting.

abbreviation see **alphabetism**

abessive see **case**

ablative see **case**

ablaut /ˈæblaʊt/ is a type of **internal modification** involving
vowels. The change in form between *sing, sang* and *sung*
is an instance of ablaut. This narrow usage where the
changes affect the forms of a verb is the most common
one. Sometimes derivational relationships between pairs
such as *fall, fell* (a tree), *rise, raise* and *sing, song* are also
included as ablaut. See also **apophony, umlaut**.

ablaut-motivated compounding refers to the juxtaposition of
word-like elements which are related to each other by a
vowel-change (**ablaut**). Words like *clip-clop, dilly-dally,
wishy-washy* illustrate the phenomenon. Note that these
are not really compounds, since they are not necessarily
made up of two independent words, and that the vowel
sounds which alternate are strictly constrained. See also
rhyme-motivated compounding.

absolutive see **case**

accusative see **case**

acronym /'ækrənɪm/ An acronym is an **alphabetism** which has the appearance of a normal word and which is pronounced as a normal word rather than as a sequence of letters. The acronym may be written as a series of capitals (as in *AIDS* 'acquired immune deficiency syndrome') or in lower case (as in *laser* 'light amplification by stimulated emission of radiation'). Marginal instances of acronyms are those items which are pronounced as words, though their orthographic form does not suggest such a pronunciation, for example, *jpg* pronounced /ˈdʒeɪpɛg/. Acronyms may shade off into **clipping compounds**.

active (1) see **voice**

active (2) is sometimes used as a synonym for **productive** or **semi-productive**, though some authorities draw distinctions between activity and productivity. See also **living**.

actual word An actual word is one which has been attested in use and typically which, in languages with a lexicographical tradition, can be found listed in a dictionary. It contrasts with a **possible** or **potential word**.

adessive see **case**

adjacency condition The adjacency condition is an attempt to explain the conditions which determine where certain affixes are or are not allowed to join on to words. The adjacency condition states that in determining whether an affix may be added to an existing structure, information about the outermost piece of the structure added may be relevant, but no material more deeply embedded may be relevant. Thus *un-* may not be added to *dishonest*, because *un-* may take account of the negativity of the adjacent element *dis-* and be blocked by it. On the other hand, the negativity of *dishonour* can no longer be relevant once an extra *-ed* is added to *dishonour*, so that *undishonoured* cannot be blocked. See also **atom condition, bracket erasure**.

adjectivalisation is the formation of adjectives by a morphological process, or a word which results from such a process. Thus the formation of *parental* by suffixation from *parent* is a process of adjectivalisation, and *parental* is an adjectivalisation.

adverbialisation is the formation of adverbs by a morphological process, or a word which results from such a process. Thus the formation of *frequently* by suffixation from *frequent* is a process of adverbialisation, and *frequently* is an adverbialisation.

affix An affix is a type of obligatorily bound **morph**. Unlike a **clitic**, an affix is attached to a base which is of a particular word-class, so that the affix *-ed*, which is used to mark the past tense in English, is attached only to verbs. Unlike an obligatorily bound root, an affix is more likely to carry functional meaning rather than lexical meaning, though it may carry both. For example, if we analyse the word *botanic* into a root *botan-* and an affix *-ic*, we see that *botan-* carries lexical meaning 'related to plants', whereas with *-ic*, the most important meaning is to specify that the new word *botanic* is an adjective, though it may also carry some lexical meaning. Only *-ic* in this example is an affix.

There are various kinds of affix, named according to

their position in relation to the **base** to which they attach. The most common are **prefix**, attached before the base, **suffix**, attached after the base, and **infix** attached inside a base. Several other types have been recognised at various times in the history of morphology. See also **circumfix, interfix, simulfix, superfix, synaffix, transfix**.

affix-ordering is concerned with the linear order in which affixes occur relative to each other in words. The rules discussed under the heading of 'affix-ordering' are concerned with the order of prefixes or the order of suffixes, rather than why something should be a prefix or a suffix. There are a number of hypotheses about the order of affixes in general or within any given language. Affix-positions may be set out in a template, where some of the positions are obligatorily filled, and others are optionally filled. Since this, in effect, stipulates the order for each language individually, it is the least predictive way of discussing order. Affixes may be ordered according to some syntactic principle, with the innermost affixes (those nearest the root) being added by syntactic processes which apply before the processes which provide the affixes further from the root. This syntactic order may or may not be related to some semantic principle: for example, it might be that affixes are ordered in terms of their relative scope, or that affixes are ordered in terms of some semantic/functional principle such as **relevance**. Finally, affixes may be ordered according to some lexical principle, so that each affix selects adjacent (usually more peripheral) affixes. **Level-ordering** presents a different approach to affix-ordering, but is not as explicit as to the precise relative ordering of individual affixes as the principles listed above have the ability to be. See also **morphotactics**.

affixation is the process of adding an **affix** to a **base**. See also **infixation, prefixation, suffixation**.

agglutinating or **agglutinative** An agglutinating language is a synthetic language where the normal pattern is for each morph to **realise** a single semantic unit or morpheme, and each morpheme to be realised by a single morph. Swahili and Turkish are often cited as clear examples of agglutinating languages. In an English sentence like *Cat·s mis·trust·ed dog·s in earli·er time·s* all the words except *in* show a basic pattern of agglutinating morphology, though the *s* on *cats* and *dogs* is pronounced differently, which would not be true in a purely agglutinating language. See also **fusional, isolating, polysynthetic**.

agreement usually means **concord**, but may also be used to mean **government** (Bloomfield).

allative see **case**

allomorph /'ælǝmɔːf/ An allomorph or 'morpheme variant' is one of the **realisations** of a **morpheme**. Allomorphs occur in complementary distribution, so that each is predictable in its environment. According to some views of the morpheme, the allomorphs also have to be phonologically similar to each other.

alphabetism An alphabetism is any sequence of letters (usually, but not always exclusively, initial letters of some phrase or title) which is used as a name or lexeme. Alphabetisms include **initialisms** and **acronyms**. The terminology in this area is not completely standardised, and 'initialism' or 'abbreviation' may be used instead of 'alphabetism'.

alternant Different allomorphs of a morpheme are sometimes termed 'morpheme alternants', especially in phonological texts. So the morpheme {knife} has two allomorphs or alternants, /naɪf/, and /naɪv/ which occurs in the plural form *knives*. These can also be termed 'stem alternants' since the morpheme which varies is a **stem** (1).

a-morphous morphology is a theory of morphology derived from **word-and-paradigm morphology,** and associated with Stephen R. Anderson. A-morphous morphology is so-called because **morphs** and **morphemes** are not fundamental units within the theory. Instead, **word-forms** are the basic building blocks, derived from lexically listed **stems** (1) and features for morphological **properties** by a number of phonological rules which create and manipulate phonological form.

analogical levelling is a process of simplification or regularisation of morphology in which an irregular or minority pattern changes to a majority or more common pattern.

analogy is the force which allows speakers to create a new construction based on an already-known parallel form. Children can create *comed* rather than *came* by analogy with *combed* and the host of other verbs which make their past tense in the same way. Most such children's analogies do not survive, but some do, for example, the use of *helped* rather than the older form *holp*.

   In a wider sense there is a debate as to whether speakers form new words by analogy with old ones or because they have acquired a rule which allows them to build new structures. That is, is a word like *witchly* (not in dictionaries but attested) formed by analogy with words like *kingly*, *manly*, *princely*, *womanly* or is it formed by a rule which says that -*ly* can be added to human nouns to create adjectives?

analysability A word is analysable to the extent that the native user of the word can perceive its morphological structure. Thus speakers of English might be expected to recognise that *unfriendly* is made up of (can be analysed into) three elements *un*-, *friend* and -*ly*. If this is the case, *unfriendly* is analysable. On the other hand, it may not be clear that *darling* is made up of *dear* and the same -*ling* element as is found in *duckling* and *princeling* (which is its history). If this is not clear, it is because *darling* is not analysable now (though it may have been so at some earlier point in time).

analytic An analytic construction is one that has separate words as its constituents. The contrary term is **synthetic**. Thus *more common* shows an analytic comparative, while *commoner* shows a synthetic comparative in English. The elements in the construction *commoner* are the base *common* and the suffix -*er*.

An analytic language is one in which constructions are generally analytic, so that morphologically complex words are rare. No language is uniformly analytic in this sense. An analytic language, one which approximates to the ideal, is also called **isolating**.

antipassive see **voice**

aorist /'eɪərɪst/ see **aspect**

apophony /ə'pɒfəni/ is a type of **internal modification** of the phonological segments of a word. Sometimes the label is used for any internal modification affecting consonants or vowels, sometimes it is used specifically for modification of vowels, and sometimes it is used even more specifically for the narrowest sense of **ablaut**.

appositional compound An appositional **compound** is one such as *maid-servant* or *fighter-bomber* in which the two elements can be seen as being equivalent in status.

aspect is a morphological category (usually marked on the verb) which provides information on the internal temporal make-up of the action denoted by that verb. Some common aspects, and their meanings, are given below.

aorist	perfective in the past tense; no longer widely used as a term.
continuous	continuing for some time; in English shown by BE + … *ing* as in *I was sitting in the car*.
habitual	happening regularly or habitually.
imperfect	progressive in the past; in English e.g. *was sitting*.
imperfective	relating to events viewed as having internal structure because being continuous, habitual, iterative, etc., like Russian *On čital pismo* 'He was reading the letter'.
inchoative	entering into a new state, starting to be something.
iterative	happening over and over again.
perfect	happening in the past but with relevance to the present; in English shown by HAVE + past participle as in *I have eaten lunch*.
perfective	relating to events viewed as wholes, like Russian *On pročital pismo* 'He read the letter' (implying that the reading was completed).

progressive   an alternative label for 'continuous' when
              used of English.
stative   being a state, i.e. something which
              endures rather than something which
              happens at a single point of time.
telic   leading to a conclusion.

See also **tense**.

atom condition The atom condition is an attempt to explain
the rules which determine where certain affixes are or are
not allowed to join on to words. The atom condition
states that in determining whether to attach (or not to
attach) an affix to an existing structure, the only relevant
information is the features which characterise the
existing structure as a whole. Thus to block *overrunned*
in favour of *overran* the feature which demands an
ablaut past tense must be a feature of the whole of
overrun. See also **adjacency condition**, **bracket erasure**.

attenuative An attenuative is an affix like the English suffix
-ish which creates *greenish* from *green*. It attenuates or
reduces in strength the meaning of the base to which it is
attached.

augmentative An augmentative is a morphological construction which is used to denote something of large size, for
example Spanish *palabrota* < *palabra* 'word'. Very often,
though not universally, augmentatives are interpreted
pragmatically as being bad or nasty in some sense, so
palabrota means not just 'large word' but 'swear word'
(compare the French expression *gros mot*: literally, 'large
word' with the same meaning). See also **diminutive**.

Autosegmental Morphology is a theory of morphology

particularly suitable for dealing with phenomena such as
reduplication and **root-and-pattern** morphology. A word
such as Arabic *katab* 'he wrote' is analysed as being
made up of a root, *ktb* meaning 'write', an active
perfective marker … *a* … *a* … , and the **binyan** is marked
by the pattern of alternation of consonants and vowels
CVCVC. The CVCVC pattern is viewed as a skeleton on
which the other morphemes are hung, each morpheme
being associated with a particular skeletal position by a
series of general rules. This is illustrated in diagrams
such as the one below, in which the Greek letter μ is used
to indicate that something is a morpheme. Note that one
result of this pattern is that the vocalic elements in this
word can be represented as a single vowel, which spreads
to fill up the empty space.

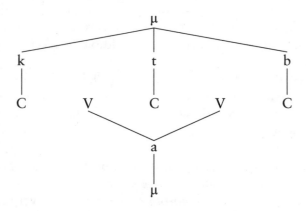

availability see **productivity**

avyayībhāva /ˈævjaɪiːˈbɑːvə/ is the name given by the Sanskrit
grammarians to an adjectival **compound** which is used
adverbially. The classification is rarely used for other
languages.

| B |

back-formation is the formation of a word by the deletion of material which either is or appears to be an affix. *Editor* was an earlier word than *edit*, which was created from *editor* by back-formation, through the deletion of *-or*; *burglar* gives rise to the verb *burgle* because the final /ə/ sounds like the agentive *-er*, though historically it is not. Back-formation is one of the major processes by which compound verbs are formed in English, for example *to baby-sit* from *baby-sitter*.

bahuvrīhi /bæhuːˈvriːhi/ is a Sanskrit word meaning 'having much rice', an example of a particular type of **compound** used as a label for that type by the Sanskrit grammarians. In Sanskrit, as the example shows, these compounds were adjectival in nature, but the label has been appropriated for English compounds of the type *greenback* ('(an American) dollar'), which is not a type of back that is green, but something which has a back which is green. This type of compound is also called a 'possessive compound', or included under the wider label of 'exocentric compound'.

base The base of a word is that part of it to which any **affix** is added or upon which any morphological process acts. In the creation of *friendly* by the suffixation of *-ly*, *friend* is the base; in the creation of *unfriendly* by the prefixation of *un-*, *friendly* is the base; in the creation of *grandmotherly*, *grandmother* is the base; in the creation of *botanic*, *botan-* is the base. Some sub-types of base are given special status in morphology, notably **roots** and **stems**.

binyan (plural: **binyanim**) /ˈbɪnjæn/ A binyan is a part of a verbal **paradigm** in a Semitic language, involving **root-**

and-pattern morphology, in which a constant pattern of consonants and vowels is maintained.

blend A blend, sometimes called a 'portmanteau word', is a word constructed from the beginning of one word and the end of another. We can distinguish at least two types. Those where either of the two blended words could occur in the same position (*smog* derives from *smoke* and *fog*, which share similar distributions) and those where both the blended words could occur (*motel* derives from *motor hotel* where *motor* is a modifier to *hotel*).

blocking is the principle invoked to account for the non-existence of one word because of the prior existence of a synonymous (or, occasionally, homophonous) word. The terms 'pre-emption by synonymy' and 'pre-emption by homophony' are sometimes used instead of 'blocking', which was introduced by Aronoff (1976). A widely cited example of blocking by synonymy is the lack of a word *stealer* in English which would be synonymous with *thief*. An example of blocking by homophony is the lack of a word corresponding to English *flier* in French, because the form *voleur*, which might appear suitable, already exists with the meaning 'thief'. Aronoff himself restricts blocking to instances where the same **base** is involved (e.g. *brevity* blocks *brevitude*), although the *stealer* example above shows that it may also be interpreted more liberally. Although blocking is discussed by Aronoff in terms of derivation, it works most obviously in inflection, where the plural **childs* is not found because of the existence of *children*, and *ran* blocks *runned*.

Without some elaboration of this fundamental explanation, many exceptions to blocking can be found.

Some scholars see blocking as part of a wider tendency for speakers to avoid synonymy. Just as synonyms are acceptable if the two words are of very different style levels or have widely differing connotations, so blocking fails to prevent the establishment of words of different style levels or with different connotations. *Childish* does not block *childlike*. The role of frequency in blocking is crucial. It is always the more frequent word which blocks the less frequent one if the two co-exist for a time. Blocking by homophony is a less strong tendency, but tends to be found where the homophony is embarrassing in some way – as with the *voleur* example above.

bound A form is obligatorily bound if it can never stand alone as a word-form, but must be attached to some other form. In the English word *musical*, *music* could be an independent word-form, but *-al* could not. *Music* is potentially free, but *-al* is obligatorily bound. (*Music* is, of course, actually bound in the word *musical*, though this is seldom taken to be of interest.) Some scholars do not use the more precise wording 'obligatorily bound' and say that *-al* is 'bound' in *musical*, but *music* is not. See also **free**.

boundary A boundary in morphology is like any other boundary: it is a dividing place. In morphology a boundary divides words or the elements of words. We can use a decimal point to note the boundaries between morphs in a word like *un·friend·li·ness*. Boundaries at the ends of words are sometimes marked with the symbol '#'. Thus a word like *give* might be shown as #give#, with boundaries included. Some theories of word-structure recognise that boundaries may have different strengths, so that some boundaries prevent certain morphophonemic processes applying between adjacent elements, while others do not. For instance, adding *-ian* to *politic* causes the final /k/ to become /ʃ/, but adding *-ing* does not. This is attributed to the kind of boundary that occurs between the elements. The strongest boundary is marked '#', and can be termed a 'double-cross boundary'. This boundary can occur inside words as well as at the ends of words, so that *politicking* would be #politic#ing# with boundaries. A weaker boundary, the one in *politician*, is marked with a '+' and can be termed a 'single-cross boundary' (sometimes, rather misleadingly, called a 'morpheme boundary'). These two boundaries correspond to the boundaries at the different levels in **level-ordering**. We can mark the boundaries in *productivity* as #productiv+ity# while *productiveness* would be #productive#ness#. The symbol '=' is used for a third, yet weaker, level of boundary when required.

bracket erasure provides a way of ordering phonological rules in morphologically complex words, and is also implicit in the **lexicalist hypothesis**. It is best explained by means of an example. Given a complex word like *[[dis [en bowel]] ment]*, the phonological and morphological merger of the material in the innermost brackets is processed first, and then those brackets and the information which depends on them are deleted to give *[[dis embowel]ment]* (where all that is known about *embowel* is that it is a verb of a particular class, and not what elements it contains or what phonological processes it has undergone), and the process starts again. This means that information about the phonology and morphology in internal brackets cannot be available to subsequent levels of affixation. At the final level, it means that words cannot be treated differentially in the syntax because of their morphological make-up. In the case in hand, the suffixation of -*ment* cannot depend on any knowledge about the prefixation of *en-*. This is not always true. See also **adjacency condition, atom condition, potentiation.**

bracketing paradox *Unhappier* means 'more unhappy' rather than 'not happier'; this implies that it is bracketed as [[unhappy]er]. The comparative -*er* suffix is easily added to disyllabic adjectives such as *pretty* (to give *prettier*), but not to trisyllabic adjectives (*shadowy* does not give rise to **shadowier*). This implies that *unhappier* must be bracketed as [un[happier]]. Two different ways of analysing the same surface form lead to different conclusions about the constituent structure of the surface form, and the two cannot be reconciled. This is a bracketing paradox.

C

case is the system of marking nouns or noun phrases to show their relationship to the verbs, prepositions or other nouns which govern them. In many languages, case is shown by affixes on nouns which indicate what their role is in the sentence: who does what to whom and with what. In the following sentence of Russian, the case markers (NOM(INATIVE), ACC(USATIVE) and INSTR(UMENTAL)) show the roles of the nouns.

moj	brat	čitajet
my.MASC.SING.NOM	brother.NOM	read.3SG.PRES

knig·u	vječer·om	
book·SING.ACC	evening·SING.INSTR	

'My brother reads the book in the evening.'

In other languages the role of nouns is indicated by their position in the sentence or by prepositions or postpositions, and linguists vary as to whether they use the term 'case' in these non-morphological contexts as well as when the relationship is shown morphologically.

The names of cases are often no more than mnemonic labels based on one of the many functions a particular case shows in a given language. For example, the Latin ablative (literally, showing movement away from) is usually glossed in English as 'by, with or from', where only the 'from' clearly deserves the label. Nonetheless, the names given to cases can be enlightening, frequently more so than in the Latin instance just cited. Some glosses are given below.

abessive	the case used to show position away from, absence of
ablative	the case used to show movement away from
absolutive	the case used for the subject of an intransitive verb and the object of a transitive verb in an ergative/absolutive system
accusative	the case used for the direct object of a verb in a nominative/accusative system
adessive	the case used to show position at (or in some languages on)
allative	the case used to show movement towards (or in some languages on to)
comitative	the case used to show 'along with, in the company of'
dative	the case for the indirect object of a verb, or (following the etymology) for the case in which the person to whom something is given occurs
direct	the direct case is contrasted with the

oblique case in a direct/oblique system. In some instances the direct case is used for the subject of the verb, and the oblique for all other roles; in other instances the direct case is used for the subject and object of the verb, but not for other roles

elative   the case used to show movement out of

ergative   the case for the subject of a transitive verb in an ergative/absolutive system

genitive   the case used to mark the possessor of something

illative   the case used to show movement into

inessive   the case used to show position within

instrumental   the case used to mark the instrument used in carrying out some action

locative   the case used to show position

nominative   the case used for the subject of a verb in a nominative/accusative system

oblique   this term has two slightly different uses. (1) In a direct/oblique system or in a nominative/oblique system, it is the marker for all roles not marked by the direct case (or nominative case). (2) In the phrase 'the oblique cases' it is used to refer to a set of cases excluding the nominative (occasionally the nominative or accusative)

partitive   the case used to show some quantity of something, e.g. in some languages in phrases equivalent to *a piece of bread* or *a pound of butter* the *of*-phrases are in the partitive case

translative   the case used to show movement across (the case may mark an intermediate point of the movement or an end point, depending on the language)

vocative   the case used when a noun is used to address someone or something

category, morphosyntactic A 'morphosyntactic' or 'morphological category' is a term used within **word-and-paradigm** morphology to refer to the kinds of features for which a particular word may be inflected. For example, in French verbs show inflection for the morphosyntactic category of Tense. However, there is no morpheme called 'tense'. The marking which is found in the word realises one of the morphosyntactic **properties** past, present or future, which belong to the category of Tense.

causative /ˈkɔːzətɪv/ A causative is the word resulting from the application of a morphological process that creates words indicating that a particular action was caused to occur. Maori *whakahaere* 'to administer, run' is the causative of *haere* 'to go', and *whaka-* is a causative prefix in this language.

cell A cell, sometimes called a 'slot', is a position in a **paradigm** defined by a combination of morphological properties. For example, in a Latin noun paradigm we expect any noun to have an accusative singular form, and so this is a cell.

checking theory is one part of Chomsky's theory of Minimalist syntax which is relevant for morphology. It is assumed that inflections on verbs exist in the syntactic tree as functional projections, and that to construct appropriate word-forms, it is necessary to check each of these functional projections against a suitable piece of morphological form, with the result that the morphs must occur in the word-form in an order corresponding to the order in which the relevant functional projections appear in the syntactic tree. Given French *donn·er·a* 's/he will give', where the *-er-* can be seen as marking futurity and the *-a* as marking third-person singular, the node dominating the verb stem must be closer to the tense node than to the person agreement node, reflecting the order of the morphs in the words. See also **mirror principle**.

circumfix   A circumfix is a type of **synaffix**. In a circumfix a prefix and a suffix together have a single unitary meaning, and the two must occur together to provide that meaning. An example of a circumfix is the *ge ... te* which derives Dutch *gebeente* 'skeleton' from *been* 'bone'.

citation form   The citation form of a **lexeme** is the form of the lexeme which is typically used when the lexeme is talked about rather than used. Accordingly it is the form of the lexeme which is listed in dictionaries. The citation form of a lexeme is conventionally determined. In English, the citation form of a verb lexeme is often its stem (e.g. *instil*); in French it is the infinitive (e.g. *demander* 'to ask'); in Latin it is the first-person singular of the present tense (e.g. *moneo* 'I warn'); in Arabic it is the masculine third-person singular past (e.g. *qatala* 'he killed').

class-changing and **class-maintaining**   A morphological process which is class-changing has a word of one word-class as its input, and a word of a different word-class as its output. If we add the suffix *-al* to the noun *person*, we end up with the adjective *personal*, and so this process is class-changing. On the other hand, if we add the suffix *-dom* to the noun *king*, we end up with another noun, *kingdom*, so this process is class-maintaining. It can be seen that the notion of 'class' involved here is not particularly subtle.

We can distinguish between affixes which are class-maintaining and affixes which are **transparent** (2) to notions of word-class. The suffix *-dom* in English always produces nouns; it just so happens that in *kingdom* (as opposed to in *freedom*) it is added to a noun, and so is class-maintaining. The Italian suffix *-ino* creates nouns when added to nouns (*tavolino* 'little table') and adjectives when added to adjectives (*giallino* 'yellowish'), for example. Both of these situations are distinct from the situation with the English prefix *counter-*, which can be added to nouns, verbs and adjectives (*countermeasure, countersign, counterintuitive*), and in each instance the word-class of the output matches the word-class of the input. Here we have no need to talk about either class-maintaining or transparent, since *counter-* is not in **head** position, and thus cannot influence the word-class.

clipping   A clipping is a word created by the removal of some material from a longer word. The removed material may come from the beginning of the word (*phone < telephone*), from the end of the word (*brill < brilliant*) or both (*flu < influenza*). A clipping means the same as the word from which it is derived, but is typically used in less formal circumstances. The process of forming clippings is also called 'clipping'.

clipping compound   A clipping compound is a **compound** in which at least one of the elements is a **clipping**. *E-mail < electronic mail, show-biz < show business* and *humint < human intelligence* are clipping compounds.

clitic   A clitic is an element which has some of the features of a word and some of the features of an inflectional affix. Like inflectional affixes, they are not independent word-forms, and they carry grammatical information. The clearest instances of clitics are reduced forms of words, like the *'ll* in *She'll be here soon*. Syntactically this behaves like a full word, but phonologically it is dependent upon *she*. Clitics like this are called simple clitics, while special clitics are forms which do not have a full-word version corresponding to *will* in the example above. An example from English is the *'s* which marks possession and can attach to whole phrases (e.g. *the candidate that we supported's problems*). Clitics which follow their bases like these are called enclitics, while those that precede their bases like the material before the verb in French *je te le donne* 'I give it to you' are called proclitics.

combining form A combining form is one of the elements which can occur in a **neo-classical compound**, but which may also occur prefixed or suffixed to a word. *Socio-* and *-ology* are combining forms, whether they occur in *sociology*, *sociolinguistics* or *musicology*. A combining form found word-initially is an 'initial combining form', one found word-finally is a 'final combining form'.

comitative /ˈkɒmɪtətɪv/ see **case**

comparative see **comparison**

comparison The comparison of adjectives is the term for the morphological category whose properties are the positive, comparative and superlative, as in *young*, *younger*, *youngest*. This category is traditionally called the category of degree.

complex A complex word is one which has morphological structure, and thus is made up of more than one morpheme. The opposing term is **simplex**. Some writers distinguish between complex and **compound**, such that complex does not include compounds, and is thus more narrowly defined than here.

composition is the process of forming **compounds**.

compound A compound is a **lexeme** which contains two (or more) **stems** (1) and which does not have any **derivational affix** which applies to the combination of stems. Thus [grand·father] is a compound while [[grand·father]ly] is a derivative whose base is a compound.

   The criteria for distinguishing between a syntactic construction and a compound are not well established, and sometimes lead to dispute as to what is or is not a compound. Possible criteria include phonological criteria (stress, vowel harmony, sandhi processes); morphological criteria (in languages which show inflection, the compound inflects as a unit for its role in the sentence); semantic criteria (there may be some degree of **lexicalisation** or idiomatisation in compounds, and also the modifying element of a compound cannot refer to particular individuals); syntactic criteria (because of the last semantic point, anaphoric forms cannot refer back to the modifying element of a compound); orthographic criteria (though whether something is written as a single **orthographic word** or more than one may depend on other factors). Any of these criteria may be used in individual languages to justify the analysis of a two-word construction as a compound.

   There is a Sanskrit classification of compounds into

avyayībhāva, bahuvrīhi, dvandva, kharmadhāraya and **tatpuruṣa** which continues to have a strong influence on modern classifications, to the point that some of the labels are still current, occasionally with slightly changed meanings. Bloomfield classified compounds into endocentric compounds (like *blackbird*, which denotes a kind of bird) and exocentric compounds (like *blackhead*, which does not denote a kind of head but something which has a head which is black, and also things like *pick-pocket*, which does not denote a kind of pocket or a kind of pick). The two are not always easy to distinguish: *lady-bird* does not denote a kind of bird, yet neither is it something which has a bird. We can also classify compounds according to whether they have a verb in their head element or not, since the interpretation of a compound with a verbal part in the head is often determined by the semantics of the verb. For example, 'primary' or 'root compounds' (better termed 'noun-centred compounds') like *windmill* are often ambiguous out of context (does the mill produce wind or is it driven by wind?), while 'synthetic' or 'verbal(-nexus) compounds' (better termed 'verb-centred compounds') like *bus-driver* tend to have a single interpretation based on the meaning of the verb (in this case *drive*).

Compounds may be nouns (*windmill*), adjectives (*red-hot*), verbs (*freeze-dry*), adverbs (*over-night, flat-stick*) or prepositions (*onto*). In some instances compound forms may arise through processes other than compounding (composition): a verb like *baby-sit* derives from the earlier *baby-sitter* by **back-formation**, while *to breath-test* arises by **conversion** from the noun *breath-test*. See also **appositional compound, coordinative compound**.

computational morphology is that branch of morphology in which computers are used to model the ways in which morphological systems work.

concord refers to a situation in which two words in a phrase or sentence both obligatorily show marking for some particular property. For example, adjectives and nouns show concord of (agree for) gender and number in Italian, so that we find *il mio zio pazzo* 'my mad uncle' but *la mia zia pazza* 'my mad aunt' where the final *-o* in *zio* and in *pazzo* shows both masculine gender and singular number. In English the verb agrees with its subject in the present tense so that we find *He fishes* but *They fish*. This is subject–verb concord.

conditioning A conditioning factor is one which demands a particular piece of behaviour or a particular form. For example, the plural suffix *-en* (with no <r> and no vowel change) occurs in standard English only in the word *oxen*. It is thus the fact that we are dealing with the **lexeme** OX which requires or conditions the use of the *-en* suffix. This suffix is lexically conditioned. The regular past tense suffix in standard English forms a full syllable only when the verb ends with a /t/ or a /d/: *wanted* and *raided*, as opposed to *cried*, *hummed*, *laughed*, *walked*, etc. This particular **allomorph** is phonologically (or phonetically) conditioned, by the sound at the end of the verb stem. The morpheme {wife} has the allomorph *wive* before plural *-s* (but not before a possessive *-'s*). This is grammatical conditioning: grammatical facts determine which form of the root will be used. Of these types of conditioning, phonological/phonetic is the one which is usually considered the most important.

conjugation see **inflection class**

connectionism In connectionist models of morphological processing, it is assumed that speakers learn both regular and irregular inflectional morphology in essentially the same way, as a set of relations in shapes between base and inflected form. Thus, though many linguists point to a difference in principle between the relationship between *go* and *went* (which holds for this lexeme only) and the relationship between *hoe* and *hoed* (which can be generalised to many other words, including new words never before heard), the connectionist claim is that they are all processed in the brain in just the same way. Computer models have been constructed which, using a system known as 'parallel distributed processing', appear to learn the correct past-tense form of English verbs given the present-tense form in just this way. The opposing view is called the **dual-route model**.

consonant mutation see **internal modification**

constructional iconicity or **diagrammaticity** Iconicity arises when form reflects meaning directly. Constructional iconicity arises when that reflection is simply a matter of quantity: a greater amount of form (measured in number of segments or, more usually, in syllables) corresponds to a greater amount of meaning. To put this another way, a process is constructionally iconic when adding material (e.g. an affix) corresponds to the addition of meaning. Thus the marking of plural in *shoe·s* is more constructionally iconic than the marking in *feet*, since making something plural is a matter of adding meaning and so needs added form to be maximally iconic. The notion has been developed within **Natural Morphology**.

content word A content word, also known as a 'lexical word', contrasts with a **function word**. The primary role of a content word is to provide the central semantic information which is grammatically linked by function words and by **inflectional** morphology. Nouns, adjectives, non-auxiliary verbs and adverbs are the basic content words.

contextual anchoring is the way in which a newly coined word is embedded in its linguistic context in such a way as to make its meaning clear. Relevant factors include glossing the new word, marking it orthographically or intonationally as being new, using it alongside synonyms or antonyms (especially ones with the same base), and so on. In the genuine example 'Candor was dangerous to both candorer and candoree', the new words *candorer* and *condoree* are introduced in contrast with each other and after the use of their base *candor*.

contextual inflection see **inflection**

continuous see **aspect**

controller In **agreement,** the controller is the element which determines the agreeing features which will occur on the **target.** If adjectives agree with nouns for number and gender, for example, as in Romance and Bantu, the noun is the controller; the subject is the controller of subject–verb agreement.

conversion is the presumed derivational process which takes place when a word which normally occurs in one word-class takes on the characteristics of a different word-class without any change of form. Thus, in isolation we would probably say that *empty* in English is an adjective, but in *Empty the bottle!* it is a verb, and in *Kim removed the* *empties* it is a noun. The latter two examples illustrate instances of conversion.

coordinative compound or **coordinate compound** are terms used for any **compounds** in which the two elements seem to be of equal standing, whether these are **dvandvas** (*Schleswig-Holstein*) where two separate entities are listed, **kharmadhārayas** (*maid-servant*) where two aspects of the same entity are listed, or other types such as Greek *xart·o·fakela* 'notepaper·LINK·envelopes' (i.e. 'stationery'), where two examples of the relevant type are put side by side, or *Latin–English dictionary*, where the two extremes are linked, or *Australian–New Zealand talks*, where participants are listed.

copulative compound see **dvandva**

cranberry morph see **unique morph**

creativity contrasts with **productivity**, and refers to the non-rule governed creation of new morphologically complex forms. Sometimes these arise by **analogy**, sometimes because they are **playful formations**, sometimes they are deliberate poetic creations. Distinguishing the outputs of creativity from the outputs of productivity may depend on the theoretical stance taken; it is not self-evident.

cumulation refers to a type of **exponence**. When two distinct semantic elements are represented by a single form, we speak of 'cumulative exponence' or 'cumulation'. For example, in the Latin *dominus* 'master' the *-us* shows the noun to be both singular and in the nominative case, and the two cannot be separated. See also **portmanteau morph**.

D

dative /ˈdeɪtɪv/ see **case**

de-adjectival means derived from an adjective. *Personalise* is a de-adjectival verb, derived from the adjective *personal*.

declension see **inflection class**

default A default is a rule that applies if no other rule has been specified as applying. In English, although there are many ways of forming the past tense of verbs, the default is to suffix -*ed*. In German, although there are very few nouns which form their plural by adding an -*s* as in *Autos* 'cars', -*s* is used where initialisms and non-nouns are made plural, for example *Abers* 'buts', so that it seems that this must be the default way of doing things. Defaults provide a way of ordering rules. See **elsewhere principle**.

defective verb A defective verb is one which does not have a complete inflectional paradigm. For example, the French verb *gésir* 'to lie', being found virtually exclusively on gravestones, is used only in the third person. The verb *clore* 'to close' appears almost only in the infinitive or past participle in modern French.

degree see **comparison**

de-nominal means derived from a noun. *Personal* is a de-nominal adjective, derived from the noun *person*.

derivation or **derivational morphology** is that type of morphology which creates new **lexemes** rather than forms of a single word (compare **inflection**). Derivational morphology is the least syntactic type of morphology:

its role is not to mark words as having particular grammatical features, but to create words from a known **base** which can fit into a different syntactic context. No syntactic construction demands the use of a word with derivational morphology (a construction such as *The ___ is black and white* works equally well with a **monomorphemic** word like *cat* in the gap or with a complex word such as *decision*), and there is not necessarily a relevant **derivative** available for every slot in a derivational **paradigm** (e.g. although *arrive* has *arrival* as its nominalisation, there is no corresponding form for *come*).

derivative A derivative is a word coined by a process of **derivation**.

desinence is a rather old-fashioned term for **inflectional affix**.

determinant /dɪˈtɜːmɪnənt/ is the label for modifier in Marchand's theory of word-formation. See also **determinatum**.

determinatum /dɪtɜːmɪˈnɑːtəm/ is the label for **head** of a word in Marchand's theory of word-formation.

de-verbal means derived from a verb. *Personification* is a de-verbal noun, derived from the verb *personify*.

diagrammaticity /daɪəɡræməˈtɪsɪti/ see **constructional iconicity**

diminutive A diminutive is a morphological construction which denotes something small, as, for example, Spanish *librito* 'booklet' < *libro* 'book'. In many languages, though not universally, diminutives are interpreted pragmatically as referring to something nice or pleasant. So Spanish *hermanita* < *hermana* 'sister' means not only a 'little sister', but something like 'dear little sister'. In many languages diminutives are used extensively in language directed at and heard from children.

direct case see **case**

discontinuous morph A discontinuous morph is one whose phonological material is kept apart by phonological material belonging to some other morpheme. **Infixation** leads to discontinuous bases, and where we find **transfixes** (or **root-and-pattern** morphology) we find both discontinuous roots and discontinuous affixes. **Circumfixes** and other **synaffixes** may be viewed as discontinuous.

disponibilité see **productivity**

distributed morphology is the name of a theory of morphology associated with Morris Halle and Alec Marantz. In this theory, syntax and morphology are treated in the same way, and what is treated in the **lexicon** in other theories is distributed across the grammar. Accordingly the **lexicalist hypothesis** is denied, as is the usefulness of constructs such as **word** and **paradigm**. The distinction between nouns and verbs is seen as being derived from the functional categories (such as determiner for nouns) which license them. Where the syntax provides fewer nodes than are required by the morphology, a process called 'fission' makes the adjustments between the two levels.

ditransitive A verb which has two objects, a direct and an indirect object, is said to be ditransitive. See also **intransitive, transitive**.

dual see **number**

dual-route model A dual-route model assumes that regular and irregular inflection are dealt with in different ways by speakers. Irregularly inflected forms such as *went* and *built* are stored and looked up in the mental lexicon. Regularly inflected forms such as *hoed* and *welded* are processed in real time, so that speakers add the affixes to the bases in the process of speaking rather than learning these forms as unanalysable wholes. There are slight variations on this basic division of labour in different versions of the model: for example, very frequent but regularly inflected forms may nevertheless be assumed to be learnt as wholes. The dual-route model has been championed especially by Steven Pinker. For the opposing view, see **connectionism**.

dvandva /ˈdvændvə/ is the name given by the Sanskrit grammarians to a type of **compound** made up of two words in a coordinated relationship. The type is infrequent in English outside a few borrowed place names (*Schleswig-Holstein*) and the names of business corporations (*Time Warner*), but is much more common in other languages such as Tamil, where the word for 'parents' is made up of the word for 'father' and the word for 'mother' in a dvandva construction. In true dvandvas like these, the names of two distinct entities are conjoined to provide the name of a new entity which is made up of the entirety of the other two. Such compounds are sometimes termed 'copulative compounds'. They need to be distinguished from a number of similar constructions, such as those illustrated in *violinist-composer*, *washer-drier*, *(the) London–Paris (train)*, *maid servant*, where the semantic relationships are not the same. See also **appositional compound, coordinative compound**.

| E |

echo word see **rhyme-motivated compound**

elative see **case**

elsewhere principle The elsewhere principle is a way of
    ordering the rules in a particular set if one of the rules
    is more general than the others. In such a set, the most
    restricted rules are ordered first, and apply if their con-
    ditions are met. If none of the restricted rules applies,
    then the most general rule will apply as a **default**. The
    most general rule thus applies in all other cases, or
    'elsewhere'.
        Suppose there is a language with three genders,
    masculine, feminine and neuter. Suppose that in this
    language, the dative plural of masculine nouns is formed
    by rule A, and the dative plural of other genders is
    formed by rule B. Rule B is more general than rule A,
    since it applies to more classes than rule A, or applies
    except where the more specific rule applies. Rule A
    will be ordered before rule B. Rule A will apply if its
    conditions are met, that is if the noun is masculine. If
    rule A does not apply, Rule B will. Rule B is therefore the
    default or 'elsewhere' rule, and rule B is ordered after
    rule A by the elsewhere principle.
        Various other names are given to the principle,
    including the 'proper inclusion principle' and 'Panini's
    principle'.

empty morph An empty morph is an element within a word
    to which no meaning can be attributed. **Interfixes** and
    thematic vowels are typical examples of empty morphs.
    Empty morphs break the expectation in morphemic
    analysis that an analysis into morphemes will be ex-

haustive, that is it will leave no element in the word which is not assigned a meaning, and no meaning in the word which is not assigned to a particular element.

enclitic see **clitic**

ending see **suffix**

endocentric /ɛndəʊ'sɛntrɪk/ see **compound**

ergative /'ɜːgətɪv/ see **case**

established An established word is one in general use in a community.

exocentric /ɛksəʊ'sɛntrɪk/ see **compound**

exponence is a term from **word-and-paradigm** morphology to denote the way in which meanings (or, more precisely, morphological **properties**) are realised by forms. For example, in the word *dogs* the final -*s* is said to be the 'exponent' of plurality. See also **cumulation, extended exponence, realisation**.

exponent see **exponence**

extended exponence is one special type of **exponence**. It is found when a particular meaning is not realised by a single piece of form, but seems to be realised by a number of pieces of form, often not contiguous to each other. Consider the forms of the Spanish verb meaning 'to love' given below:

| amo | 'I love' |
| amamos | 'we love' |

aman	'they love'
amaban	'they loved'
amabamos	'we loved'
amaremos	'we will love'
amaran	'they will love'

Consider, in particular, the form *amaremos* 'we will love'. The stem is *am-*, the *-ar* marks the future (and in the third-person plural is the only marker of the future), the *-mos* marks first-person plural, but the *-e* also marks the future, since in the present tense and the preterite we would find *-a* in the same position. Thus both the *-ar* and the *-e* mark futurity, and we have extended exponence. See also **cumulation**.

$\boxed{\text{F}}$

feature percolation see **percolation**

feminine see **gender**

final combining form see **combining form**

finite is used of verbs to mean 'referring to a limited period of time', and is thus often equivalent to 'tensed'. In more general terms, finite is used of any verb that could stand alone as the main verb in a sentence.

first person see **person**

f-morpheme is a term from **distributed morphology** for a morpheme which is attached to a functional node. See also **function word, l-morpheme**.

folk etymology or **popular etymology** is a form of morphological reanalysis whereby speakers perceive a morphologically unanalysable word as containing at least one recognisable component. Loan words seem particularly susceptible to folk etymology: French *femelle* with no relation to *male* is analysed in English as *female*, Spanish *cucuracha* is analysed as having something to do with male birds in *cockroach*, and *woodchuck* is derived from a native north American name that has nothing to do with throwing timber. See also **reanalysis**.

form A form is anything which has a physical shape, be that in terms of sound-waves or written characters. **Morphology** is the study of form (Greek *morphē* 'form, shape'), but in relation to meaning. In morphology, *form* refers specifically to those accretions of material (speech sounds or letters) which act as units in the construction of words. The adjective from 'form' is 'formal', and a formal distinction is a distinction of form.

formative Formative is one of those terms which is defined differently by different authors. It can mean at least the following different things:

(i)   a **morpheme**;
(ii) a morpheme specifically in the sense used by Aronoff (Bauer);
(iii) the form representing a morpheme or the **cumulated** expression of many morphemes;
(iv) an element of a word, independent of whether it has or does not have any recognisable meaning.

The term 'formant' is sometimes found with the same meaning, though this is rare.

fourth person see **person**

free A form is said to be potentially free if it has the ability to stand as an independent **word-form,** but to be obligatorily **bound** if it does not have this possibility. In the word *arising, arise* is potentially free, since *arise* could be a word-form, but *-ing* is obligatorily bound because it does not have this possibility. (Note that no attention has been paid here to the spelling of *arise*, whose final <e> is missing in *arising*. Note also that *arise* is actually bound in the word *arising*, though still potentially free.) Some scholars do not use the more precise wording 'potentially free' and refer to *arise*, even in *arising*, as being 'free'.

frozen see **institutionalisation**

full-entry theory A full-entry theory is any theory in which all morphologically complex words in any language are listed in their entirety in the speaker's **lexicon**. This is opposed to theories in which speakers are presumed to perform morphological operations as they speak or listen, creating or interpreting the relevant morphological structure.

function word A function word, also called a 'grammatical word', contrasts with a **content word**. A function word has as its primary role the marking of grammatical function. Examples are articles, prepositions, auxiliary verbs.

functional shift see **conversion**

fusional A fusional language is a **synthetic** language in which, for some significant part of the inflectional morphology, it is not possible to isolate a morph to correspond to every semantic unit which can be distinguished in the word-form. The Classical languages Latin, Greek and Sanskrit are often cited as good examples of fusional languages, which are sometimes referred to as 'inflecting' or 'inflectional' languages. In an English sentence like *Those were stolen*, each word can be argued to show fusional morphology: *those* because it contains the ideas of 'that' and 'plural', and we cannot analyse it neatly into two parts, *were* because it contains the notions of 'be' and 'past tense' and 'plural subject', and *stolen* because it contains the notions of 'steal' and 'past participle'. In the terminology of **word-and-paradigm** morphology, which is designed to cope with fusional languages, these languages show various complex patterns of **exponence**. See also **agglutinating, isolating, polysynthetic**.

future see **tense**

future participle A **participle** which is morphologically marked as belonging to the future **tense** is a future participle. English has no future participles, but they are found in Latin.

G

gender is a morphological category which divides nouns into classes on the basis of the sex of the objects typically referred to by nouns in that class. So a class which contains most of the nouns referring to male beings is called 'masculine', a class which contains most of the nouns referring to female beings is called 'feminine' and a class which contains mainly nouns not referring to sexed creatures may be termed 'neuter'. It is important to note that many of the nouns in the masculine gender will not refer to male beings, but the label is still used; equally, occasionally nouns in other genders may refer to male beings. In some language the term 'gender' is used by analogy with such systems, even where there is no fundamental link with sex. The gender of a noun is recognised by the **concord** of other elements with the noun. It follows that a language which does not show concord does not have gender. The term 'gender' is sometimes used interchangeably with **noun class**.

generalisation An affix or morphological process is said to be 'generalised' to the extent that it can be observed in the **established** vocabulary of a language. That is, generalisation is the reflection of past profitability. See also **productivity**.

genitive see **case**

gerund see **participle**

gerundive see **participle**

gloss A gloss is the element-by-element translation of linguistic data, which shows the morphological properties in each word-form. Typically the properties are glossed using abbreviations in small capitals, while lexemes are glossed using lower-case words. Words of the original are aligned with their glosses. The elements are separated where applicable in the original words (and correspondingly in the glosses) with the decimal point or, more usually, with a hyphen. Where there is cumulation, the various elements are separated either by full stops (periods) or by equals-signs. A typical three-line gloss of some data is shown below, the third line being the free translation of the material into English. It may occasionally be necessary to give a four-line gloss where the original language has complex morpho-phonemics, as the shape of the morphs may not be easily deducible from the expected underlying morphemic shape.

Danish

Lær·er·en·s	kone	rejse·r	til
teach·AGT·DEF·GEN	wife	travel·PRES	to

ud·land·et	forgæves
out·country·DEF	in.vain

'The teacher's wife travels abroad in vain'

government refers to a situation where one word in a sentence determines the form of another. In traditional grammatical terminology, a preposition or a verb is said to 'take' the dative, for example. These are instances of government, where the preposition or the verb determines the case of a grammatically related noun.

grammatical word (1) A grammatical word is a word defined in morphological terms by its place in an inflectional **paradigm**. If we consider a Latin noun paradigm such as that for DOMINUS 'lord', as set out below, we find that the **form** *dominī* appears in several **cells** in the paradigm.

DOMINUS 'lord'	Singular	Plural
Nominative	dominus	dominī
Vocative	dominē	dominī
Accusative	dominum	dominōs
Genitive	dominī	dominōrum
Dative	dominō	dominīs
Ablative	dominō	dominīs

Each of the forms *dominī* in this paradigm represents a different grammatical word, although the **word-forms** are homophonous (some might say identical), and although we are dealing with a single **lexeme**. These different grammatical words are described by labels such as 'the genitive singular of DOMINUS' which define the relevant cell in the paradigm.

A grammatical word in this sense is sometimes called a 'morphosyntactic word'.

grammatical word (2) A grammatical word is a word defined in terms of its morphology and syntax as a unit showing internal cohesion. Internal cohesion is usually defined in terms of positional mobility (the word may occur in different positions in the syntactic string), uninterruptability (the word cannot be freely interrupted with material from elsewhere in the sentence) and internal stability (the order of **morphs** within the word is fixed and non-contrastive) (Lyons). These various criteria are not universally met in full, with **fusional** languages tending to show greatest positional mobility (sometimes called 'scrambling' by syntacticians) and **agglutinating** languages showing lowest internal stability. Nevertheless, together these criteria define what has also been called a 'syntactic atom' (Di Sciullo and Williams 1987).

A grammatical word in this sense is sometimes called a 'morphosyntactic word'.

grammatical word (3) see **function word**

grammaticalisation or **grammaticisation** Although grammaticalisation may arise in many areas besides morphology, one of the areas where it has great influence is morphology. Grammaticalisation deals with the way in which grammatical structures develop historically from lexical structures or pragmatic structures. For example, the morphs which mark future tense are very often descended historically from words for volition, ability, motion towards, intention and possession. Thus, the final -*a* in the French third-person-singular future tense form *donnera* 's/he will give' derives historically from a form of the verb meaning 'to have', compare modern French *Elle a un frère* 'She has a brother'. In English *will come*, the *will* has not become an affix, but still arises from a statement of volition. The slogan for grammaticalisation studies, from Talmy Givón, is that 'today's morphology is yesterday's syntax'. While this is not universally true, it is true enough to be interesting.

H

habitual see **aspect**

hapax legomenon (plural: **hapax legomena**) /ˈhæpæks lɪˈɡɒmənɒn/ A hapax legomenon, or simply a 'hapax', is a word which occurs once only in a given text or corpus. The corpus may be an electronic text archive, or it may be the records for an entire language such as Classical Greek. In recent times the frequency of hapax legomena in a corpus has been used to calculate the **productivity** of affixes or morphological processes.

head The notion of head in morphology is a generalisation of a syntactic notion, and applies most easily in the places that most resemble syntax. In a compound such as English *body-louse* or German *Haus·frau* 'housewife' the second element is the head of the construction because (i) the word as a whole is a hyponym of its head (a body-louse is a type of louse – see also **is a condition**);

(ii) the second element determines the gender and/or inflection class of the compound as a whole (the plural of *body-louse* is *body-lice* because the plural of *louse* is *lice*; *Hausfrau* is feminine because *Frau* is feminine and despite the fact that *Haus* is not); (iii) the second element determines that the compound is a noun rather than an adjective or a verb (this is a generalisation of point (ii)); (iv) the second element carries the inflections which apply to the compound as a whole; (v) the second element is obligatory while the first element could be omitted. This much is uncontroversial. However, when we look at other morphological constructions, things are not quite as simple. When it comes to derivational morphology such as is shown in *hopefulness*, *-ness* is generally taken to be the head of the word by criteria (iii) and (iv) above. In *foretell*, *tell* is the head by criteria (ii), (iii) and (iv). This is sometimes generalised as the **right-hand head rule**. In inflectional morphology such as is shown in *tells* or French *donn·er·i·ons* 'we would give' things are even less clear, and often the right-hand head rule is generalised to make the last suffix the head of the word as a whole, though some scholars prefer not to see inflectional affixes as heads, so that *tell* and *donn-* would be the heads in the examples here. Under this theory, it might be argued that inflectional affixes are **transparent** (2) with regard to word-class, and that they do not mark it themselves.

hortative see **mood**

hypocoristic /ˌhaɪpəʊkəˈrɪstɪk/ A hypocoristic is a pet-name, such as *Liza*, *Liz*, *Lizzy*, *Libby* or *Beth* from *Elizabeth*. Hypocoristics may give evidence of productive patterns of shortening and embellishing words, as with *Shazza* from *Sharon*, but more often they are remnants of old shortening processes which are no longer productive, or remnants of children's mispronunciations of names. They nevertheless may share features with **diminutives,** which also feature frequently in nursery language.

I

IA see **item and arrangement**

idiom An idiom is any sequence of words whose meaning cannot be computed from the meanings of its parts. Phrasal verbs like *put down* 'kill', and phrases like *bite the bullet* 'face up to something unpleasant' are idioms. While the term 'idiom' is less often used of complex words, the same principles may apply, so that *blackmail* and *(your) highness* cannot be understood on the basis of an understanding of their elements. In **distributed morphology,** even the meanings of roots is seen as idiomatic. See also **lexicalisation.**

idiomatisation /ˌɪdɪəmətaɪˈzeɪʃən/ is the formation of an **idiom** or the making of something into an idiom, and is the semantic aspect of **lexicalisation.**

illative see **case**

imperative see **mood**

imperfect see **aspect**

imperfective see **aspect**

inchoative /ɪŋˈkəʊətɪv/ see **aspect**

incorporating An incorporating language is one that uses **incorporation.**

incorporation is a particular type of **compounding** (in that it involves two different lexemes) where a noun or adverb is built into the word which functions as the verb in a sentence. Thus in a language like Nahuatl, there is a difference between the equivalents of *I eat the meat* 'I am in the process of consuming some particular piece of meat' and *I meat-eat* 'I am a carnivore', where the incorporated object in the second example is non-specific (it is not possible to ask 'which meat?') and the meaning is general. The nearest English gets to incorporation is in compounds like *baby-sitting*, *fox-hunting*, which have similar semantics but where the process is very much more restricted than in typical incorporating languages. See also **polysynthetic**.

indeclinable A word which is indeclinable is one which has a fixed form despite the fact that other comparable words show different forms in different cells of the **paradigm**.

indicative see **mood**

inessive see **case**

infinitive /ɪnˈfɪnɪtɪv/ The infinitive is a non-finite or untensed form of the verb. In English and French, among other languages, the infinitive is the **citation form** of the verb. In English the infinitive is either cited as a bare stem (*do*, *walk*) or with the preceding marker *to* (*to do*, *to walk*).

infix /ˈɪnfɪks/ An infix is an affix which interrupts the morph to which it is added (usually the root of the word). In Khmer, /suo/ means 'to ask' and /sɔmnuo/ means 'question'. The /ɔmn/ which changes the verb into a noun is inserted into the middle of the morph meaning 'ask' (neither /s/ nor /uo/ mean anything in isolation), and is an infix. By contrast, the difference between *donn·a* 's/he gave' and *donn·er·a* 's/he will give' in French is that the former has a single suffix, while the latter has two. The *-er-* comes between two morphs, but does not interrupt either morph, and so is not an infix.

infixation is the addition of an **infix** to a **base**.

inflecting see **fusional**

inflection or **inflectional morphology** is the morphology which provides different forms of the same word to show the role that word plays in a sentence. These different forms are traditionally set out as a **paradigm**. Inflectional morphology is the most syntactically relevant type of morphology, which is obligatory in a particular syntactic construction and which typically has a form associated with every cell in the paradigm.

Inflection can be divided into 'contextual' inflection, which is the morphology demanded by the construction in which the word occurs (e.g. adjectives agreeing with nouns in Italian, verbs agreeing with subjects in many European languages, nouns taking particular **cases** depending on the verbs or prepositions that govern them), and 'inherent' inflection, which is the inflectional morphology that is not due to agreement, but which is usually chosen independent of the syntactic construction (e.g. **tense** on verbs in French and many other languages, **comparative** on adjectives in most constructions).

The **affixes** which are added to stems for inflectional morphology are also called inflections.

See also **derivation**.

inflection class or **inflectional class** An inflection class is a set of words which show the same inflectional morphology. For example, *drive, drove, driven* and *ride, rode, ridden* belong to the same inflectional class in English. Inflection classes for verbs are usually called 'conjugations', while inflection classes for nouns are usually called 'declensions'.

inflectional see **fusional**

inflectional class stability is a notion from **Natural Morphology**. It refers to the tendency for **inflectional classes** to become more consistent in the forms they show over time. For example, German masculine nouns seem to be changing slowly to lose plurals that end in *-n* while feminine nouns are gaining *-n* plurals because most feminine nouns already have *-n* plurals, and most masculine ones do not.

inherent inflection see **inflection**

initial combining form see **combining form**

initialism An initialism is an **alphabetism** made up of the initial letters of the phrase for which it stands, and pronounced as a sequence of letters. *BBC* /biː biː siː/ is an initialism for *British Broadcasting Corporation*.

institutionalisation is a step along the way to **lexicalisation**. In principle, many complex words are multiply ambiguous. If we had never met the word *beater* before, for example, we would not know whether it was a person or a machine. In this case it has become institutionalised with the two different meanings, one in the domain of hunting, one in the domain of the kitchen. The acceptance of one meaning in a particular domain within a community tends to prevent the acceptance of the alternative meaning in the same domain (see **blocking**). The moment the meaning is established in the community, the word is said to be institutionalised. An institutionalised word is sometimes called 'frozen' or 'petrified'.

instrumental see **case**

interfix An interfix is an **affix** which occurs between two elements, linking them together. Interfixes are also termed 'linking elements'. In German *Liebesbrief* 'love letter', -*s*- is an interfix between *Liebe* 'love' and *Brief* 'letter'. Interfixes may be descended from inflectional markers, but they typically show no meaning of their own and may be classed as **empty morphs**. An alternative analysis which is always available is to see the presumed interfix as belonging to the morph on one or the other side, and creating a new **allomorph** for the relevant **morpheme**.

internal cohesion is the defining characteristic of a **grammatical word** (2).

internal modification is any change to the phonological make-up of a **base** which has a semantic effect equivalent to adding some **affix**. For instance, the change in the vowel from *foot* to *feet* has the same effect as adding an affix to *hand* to give *hands*. This is one type of internal modification. We can distinguish several sub-types.

First there are changes of vowels, like the one illustrated in *foot* and *feet*. Different sub-types of vocalic alternation or 'vowel mutation' are distinguished, depending on their historical origin. See **ablaut, umlaut**. Where the vowels in a word act quasi-independently of the consonants in giving meanings as in Arabic *katab* 'he wrote', *kitaab* 'book', *kaatib* 'clerk' (where the root is **ktb*, indicating 'writing'), the vocalic changes are sometimes discussed as internal modification (sometimes using the label **apophony**), and, in older texts, referred to as **transfixes**. See also **root-and-pattern**.

Consonantal changes or 'consonant mutation' can be illustrated from English, with the noun–verb pairs *belief–believe*, *sheath–sheathe*, *house–house* (/haʊs-haʊz/). In each case the noun ends in a voiceless fricative, the verb in the corresponding voiced fricative. Such changes are sometimes included under **apophony**.

Changes in stress such as distinguish the English noun–verb pairs '*import–im'port*, '*transfer–trans'fer* illustrate a different type of internal modification.

Tonal changes can also be used to mark morphological relationships, as in the following examples from Cantonese:

Verb	Tone	Gloss	Noun	Tone	Gloss
taːm	53	'carry'	taːm	44	'burden'
sow	53	'count'	sow	44	'number'

In the older literature, such changes in stress and intonation were sometimes referred to as 'superfixes' or 'suprafixes'.

internal stability is one of the criteria for internal cohesion in the definition of a **grammatical word** (2). It means that the order of the morphs within a word is fixed and non-contrastive.

intransitive A verb which has no direct object is said to be intransitive. See also **ditransitive, transitive**.

intransitiviser An intransitiviser is a morphological element which marks a changed status from **transitive** to **intransitive**.

introflection /ˌɪntrəˈflɛkʃən/ see **root-and-pattern**

inversion is the phenomenon of affixes which mark one thing in one part of a paradigm marking something different (perhaps the opposite) in another part of the paradigm. Thus in Potawatomi the verbal prefix *k-* marks second-person subject except where there is a third-person subject; then *k-* shows second-person object.

IP see **item and process**

is a condition This is a name given to the condition of hyponymy in endocentric **compounds**. If we consider a compound like *godchild*, we see that a godchild is a child and not a god. In other words, *godchild* is a hyponym of *child*. This condition says that the compound is a hyponym of its head element or a godchild *is a* child.

isolating An isolating language is one in which, as a general pattern, each word corresponds to a single semantic unit. Correspondingly, no word of an ideal isolating language would ever be made up of two or more morphs. No language is completely isolating, though Vietnamese and Classical Chinese are often cited as being close to the notional ideal. An English sentence such as *Let the dog see the rabbit* shows isolating morphology, in that no word is morphologically complex. Isolating languages are sometimes called **analytic** languages. See also **agglutinating, fusional, polysynthetic**.

item and arrangement, abbreviated as IA, is a structuralist model of morphology. In this model, the items (the morphs) are listed and the rules specify the ways in which they are arranged. The difference in marker for the third-person-singular present tense in words like *blushes* and *calculates* is handled by saying there are two items meaning 'third-person-singular present tense', /ɪz/ which occurs only after the sounds /s, z, ʃ, ʒ, tʃ, dʒ/ and /s/ which occurs only after voiceless sounds not in the first list. See also **item and process, word-and-paradigm**.

item and process, abbreviated as IP, is a structuralist model of morphology. In this model, items (morphemes) are specified in a basic or underlying form, and other allomorphs are derived from that underlying form by a number of phonological processes. Generative phonology as practised by Chomsky and Halle was basically a version of IP morphology. The allomorphs of the third-person-singular present tense in English, are derived from an underlier, probably /z/, which is the most widely distributed allomorph, and the /ɪz/ in *blushes* and the /s/ in *calculates* are derived from that by vowel insertion and devoicing respectively. See also **item and arrangement, underlier, word-and-paradigm**.

item familiarity refers to a process of **institutionalisation**. A word is item-familiar if that particular word is known to speakers in the speech-community. Compare **type familiarity**.

iterative /'ɪtərɪtɪv/ see **aspect**

J

jussive /'dʒʌsɪv/ is an old term for imperative (see **aspect**).

K

kharmadhāraya /ˌkɑːməˈdɑːrɪə/ is a sub-type of **tatpuruṣa compound** in the Sanskrit classification. There are two sub-types of kharamadhāraya: those that are made up of an adjective and a noun, like *whiteboard*, and those where the two nouns in the compound each refer to some aspect of the same entity. These are compounds such as *maid servant, washer-drier*, which are sometimes mistakenly classified as **dvandva** compounds.

L

lemma (plural: **lemmata**) /ˈlɛmə/ is a term used particularly by lexicographers and corpus linguists to refer to a word in all its inflectional and spelling forms. A word-list from a text is said to be lemmatised when all the **word-forms** are associated with their **lexemes**. As well as word-forms, alternative spellings might also be involved, so that *judgment* and *judgement* might be lemmatised as the same entity. 'Lemma' is another word for a headword in a dictionary (on the assumption that each part of speech demands a new headword).

level-ordering is a theoretical principle called on to explain **affix-ordering**, morphophonemic effects over affix boundaries, and the varying effect of stress in morphologically complex words. In English, and a number of other languages, affixes can be assigned to one of two classes, more or less corresponding to distinct etymological origins of affixes (in English, whether they come from Germanic stock, or whether they are borrowed from Latin or Romance). The claim in level-ordering is that these two classes are ordered in relation to each other and that they have consistent and distinct phonological effects. This is illustrated in the following table.

	Class I/Level I affixes	Class II/Level II affixes
Examples:	-al]_A,[1] -ation, -ic, -ify, -ity	-dom, -er, -ing, -ish, -ness, -ship
A: Class I affixes occur closer to the root than Class II affixes	*musicalness*	**reddishity*
B: Only Class I affixes can be attached directly to obligatorily bound roots	*dental*	**dentish*
C: Class II affixes never affect the stress of the base to which they are attached; Class I affixes may make such a change	'parent > pa'rental	'parent > 'parentish
D: Class I affixes may cause some morphophonemic changes which are not caused by Class II affixes	/mə'laɪn/ > /mə'lɪgnɪti/ (*malign > malignity*)	/mə'laɪn/ > /mə'laɪnə/ (*malign > maligner*)

There is growing evidence that, at least for English, this correlation of phonological and morphological facts is not as straightforward as this presentation suggests.

lexeme /'lɛksiːm/ is the technical term used for one of the meanings of **word**. In English we might want to say that *came*, *come*, *comes*, *coming* are all the same word, or we might want to say that they are all different words. In the sense in which they are the same word, we use the term

---

1. That is, the *-al* suffix that creates adjectives, as in *parental*, rather than the one that creates nouns as in *arrival*.

'lexeme'. Although notation is variable from one scholar to the next, the most common convention is to mark lexemes in small capitals (Lyons), so that we can say that *come* (along with *came*, *comes* and *coming*) is one of the forms of (the lexeme) COME. Some scholars reserve the term 'lexeme' for items that can be realised by a number of different forms, like COME, others use the term to show a certain level of abstraction, and for them there is a lexeme BETWEEN. See also **citation form, lemma, word-form**.

lexeme-formation This term is used by some scholars to replace **word-formation** when they want to stress that inflectional morphology is excluded from consideration, or be precise about what kind of **word** is intended.

lexical (1) means 'of or relating to lexemes'. This sense is used if it is said that sex is marked lexically in English in the words *stallion* and *mare*, or in the expression 'lexical conditioning'. (2) 'Lexical' also means 'of or relating to the lexicon'. It is used in this sense in the terms 'lexical item' and 'lexicalisation'.

lexical entry A lexical entry is the hypothetical listing of a particular lexical item in the **lexicon**. This is assumed minimally to include all the information about the **lexical item** which is unpredictable, such as its form and its meaning (since these are assumed, following Saussure, to be arbitrary and conventional). In some languages noun- and verb-class may equally be unpredictable, and thus part of the lexical entry.

lexical generality is a principle invoked by Joan Bybee to explain **affix-ordering** and the distinction between **inflection** and **derivation** cross-linguistically. Lexical generality refers to the number of potential bases a particular category can be applied to. For example, the relationship captured by the prefix *step-* in English can apply to relatively few nouns (*mother, father, parent, child, son, daughter*, etc.), while the plural relationship can apply to many. Thus plural, being more lexically general, is more likely to arise as an inflectional category than the *step*-relationship, not only in English, but across languages. See also **relevance**.

lexical item A lexical item or 'listeme' is something which is entered in the **lexicon**. Morphologists argue as to whether **morphemes** are listed in the lexicon, but it is assumed that **simplex** lexemes are. Whether all **complex** lexemes are listed is controversial, since lexemes may be coined on the spot as **nonce forms**, and in such cases it is not clear that they can be listed. For some scholars, none of the lexemes formed by the most **productive** processes are listed. However, there are also things larger than lexemes which must be listed in the lexicon because the relation between form and meaning cannot be predicted by general rule. These include at least phrasal verbs (like *put up with* 'support, bear', *let down* 'disappoint', *look up* 'search for; start to improve') and idioms (like *kick the bucket* 'die', *red herring* 'irrelevancy'), and so on. Some scholars believe that lexical items include syntactic constructions with gaps in, such as *It BE NUMBER past NUMBER* (giving rise to *It was twenty past seven* etc.), *NOUN PHRASE BE as thick as two short planks*, *All NOUN PHRASE HAVE to do is ask*.

See also **lexical entry**.

Lexical Morphology is a theory of morphology in which the phonological behaviour of affixes is tied closely to their morphological behaviour. One example of this close relationship is **level-ordering**. (Although Lexical Morphology need not imply level-ordering, the two often go together.) Lexical Morphology is sometimes called 'Lexical Phonology' or 'Lexical Phonology and Morphology'.

lexical word see **content word**

lexicalisation is the process of becoming less **transparent** (1) and fusing into an unanalysable word. As a morphologically complex word becomes more familiar with use, its internal structure becomes less important for the speaker or listener. It is no longer necessary to realise that *stealth* is related to *steal* or *birth* to *bear* (children) in order to use it appropriately. At this point it is possible for the pronunciation of the elements in the complex word to undergo changes which are different from those undergone by the elements in isolation, so that *stealth* no longer has the same vowel as *steal*, for example. At some point it becomes impossible to recognise the elements as being the same as the original forms, and a new morpheme has formed. For example, the word *lord* once had two elements in it corresponding to *loaf* and *ward* ('guardian'). *Lord* is no longer transparently analysed into these elements, but is lexicalised. The process of lexicalisation is a gradual one, and the point at which something is lexicalised may be contentious. One suggestion is that something is lexicalised when it would not be produced by currently **productive** rules. See also **idiomatisation, institutionalisation**.

lexicalist hypothesis The lexicalist hypothesis states that no rule of syntax can depend on or make reference to any internal element or structure of a word. Thus given *hospitalise*, we cannot make *hospital* plural and get *hospitalsise* (because pluralising is something that interacts with syntax) and we cannot use a syntactic element such as *it* to refer to *hospital* in this word. Consider an example such as *Chomskyans think that he is right about the innateness of grammar.* If it is possible for *he* to refer to *Chomsky*, this sentence breaks the lexicalist hypothesis, because *Chomsky* occurs internally in the word *Chomskyans*. Examples like this which contain proper names provide some of the rare exceptions to the hypothesis.

lexicon The lexicon is the dictionary which is assumed to exist either in the heads of speakers or as a social construct shared by speakers of a single language variety. It is not a physical book, and it is not arranged like a physical dictionary. It allows access through multiple routes such as form and meaning (rather than simply in terms of alphabetical order like a physical dictionary) and it contains much more information than a normal dictionary, for instance, information on the grammatical and lexical patterns which particular listed items can enter into. There is theoretical dispute about precisely what is in the lexicon, whether it is only information which cannot be predicted by general rule, or whether some rule-governed behaviour can also produce material which is lexically listed. For some writers, all morphological operations are lexical, for others only **derivational morphology** and **compounding** are lexical, and, for some, **productive** patterns of derivation and compounding may not be lexical. There is also dispute as to the form of information in the lexicon: is it purely generalisations over listed items, is it just links between individual listed items, or is it also statements of how to make new items which could then be listed?

linking element see **interfix**

listeme see **lexical item**

living is a term sometimes used for 'available', see **productivity**.

l-morpheme is a term from **distributed morphology** for a morpheme with lexical content. See also **content word**, **f-morpheme**.

locative see **case**

M

marked (1) A morphological property is marked if it has a **marker** showing its presence. Thus the English past tense is marked in words like *walked*, but the present tense in *walk* is not marked. This sense of 'marked' is translated into German as *merkmalhaft*, sometimes rendered as 'markered' in English. (2) From this derives a related meaning where 'marked' is nearly the opposite of **natural**. This sense is called *markiert* in German. A morphological phenomenon is marked in this sense if (i) it is rare in the languages of the world, (ii) it regularly disappears in instances of language change, (iii) it is acquired relatively late by children, (iv) it is subject to errors in speech production and is attacked early by aphasias and (v) it is rare in the languages in which it occurs. A category of dual (see **number**), for example, is marked in relation to the category of plural: many languages have a plural marker but no dual marker, dual vanishes relatively easily in language change (as it has in English); it is a complex notion in those languages which have it, used relatively rarely and thus acquired relatively late. Marked categories are often subject to **syncretisms** which hide them (especially in marked environments – so dual and plural might have an identical marker in a relatively rare case form, for example) or have phonologically bulky markers. See also **unmarked**.

marker A marker is anything which indicates the presence of a morphological **property**, typically an **affix** or the like.

markered see **marked**

masculine see **gender**

masdar /ˈmæzdɑː/ A masdar is the name given in the description of some languages to a de-verbal noun created by inflection.

metathesis /mɛˈtæθəsɪs/ is a phonological process by which adjacent sounds switch position. For example, in English *waps* and *wasp* have long existed side-by-side, with *waps* probably the older form in English. In some languages, however, metathesis is used as a morphological process. Clallam, a native American language from the Pacific coast, is often cited in this regard. There /tʃkʷut/ 'shoot' and /tʃukʷt/ 'shooting' are related in the same way as /mtəqʷt/ 'put in water' and /mətqʷt/ 'putting in water'. In each case there is metathesis of the consonant vowel sequence immediately following the initial consonant of the base.

middle see **voice**

mirror principle This principle states that the order of affixes in a word directly reflects the order of the syntactic derivation. See also **affix-ordering, checking theory, morphotactics**.

modality is the expression of certainty, possibility, probability, obligation and necessity. See **mood**.

moneme /ˈməʊniːm/ Moneme is the anglicisation of the French word *monème*, which is used by French linguists, following Martinet, as a term more or less equivalent to English **morpheme**.

monomorphemic /mɒnəʊmɔːˈfiːmɪk/ means containing only one morpheme, thus having no morphological structure. *Elephant* and *go* are both monomorphemic words in English.

mood is a morphological category (usually marked on the verb) which shows, among other things, a speaker's commitment to what is said. Precisely what is covered by 'mood' may differ from one language to another. Some typical moods and their meanings are given below.

hortative	shows exhortation
imperative	expresses a direct command
indicative	shows a normal statement
subjunctive	shows subordination, unreality, or desire

Mood often overlaps with **modality** (and the two labels may be used interchangeably in some languages), so that mood can also show obligation, necessity, probability and the like.

morph A morph is a segment of a **word-form** which **realises** a **morpheme**. Morphs are **forms** established in such a way that every segment in a word-form belongs to one and only one morph. In *unfriendly* the morphs are *un*, *friend* and *ly*. The decimal point may be used to divide a word-form into morphs in writing unless superseded by orthographic hyphens: *un·friend·ly* (Bauer).

morpheme /'mɔːfiːm/ Although the morpheme is the fundamental unit of morphology, it is given a wide range of definitions, some of which appear to be trying to capture the same concept, others of which clearly define a different unit. At the extremes, some scholars deny the validity of the notion completely. Recently, the notion of morpheme has been constrained by the notion of **morphome**, which takes over some of the area previously covered by some of the definitions of the morpheme. Here, some of the different definitions of the morpheme will be given, and their implications considered.

The term was apparently invented by Baudouin de Courtenay in about 1880, though not given a very precise definition at first. For Bloomfield a morpheme is 'a linguistic form which bears no partial phonetic-semantic resemblance to any other form' and an 'ultimate constituent'. Note that here the morpheme is defined as a **form** (and so is what we later come to call a **morph**). But for other linguists forms with the same meaning which occur in complementary distribution are taken to represent the same morpheme (for instance, Harris – who talks of 'morpheme alternants' being grouped together as morphemes). A different and more widespread terminology for 'morpheme alternants' calls the -*en* in *oxen* and the -*s* in *cows* **allomorphs** of the same morpheme (for Bloomfield, they would have been synonymous morphemes). While the forms in which a morpheme can occur can differ (slightly, as in *knife* and *knives*, or even radically as in *go* and *went*), the meaning associated with the forms has to remain the same if they are to count as the same morpheme. The definitions from scholars such as Hockett and Nida give this side of the morpheme priority: morphemes become, in Hockett's terms, 'minimum meaningful elements' – a type of definition still used by some scholars today. Aronoff, on the other hand, has tried to redefine the morpheme with a formal side as an alternative to a meaning side. Given sets like *commit–commission, remit–remission; conceive–conception, receive–reception*, he points out that even though it may not be possible to state a meaning for *-mit* or *-ceive* which will hold in all relevant words, yet precisely the set of words with that element in them have a particular irregular nominalisation. Despite the fact that he admits there is no common meaning involved, Aronoff calls this element a 'morpheme', on the grounds that it has variants which look similar to allomorphs: *mit* and *miss, ceive* and *cept*.

Within early generative grammar, the term 'morpheme' was given yet another meaning. It was used as the label for the kind of syntactic feature which influences the form in which individual **words** occur. This is rather like Lyons's definition of the morpheme as 'the minimal unit of grammatical analysis' (whose origins can clearly be seen in Bloomfield's definition given above), or even like the French meaning of *morphème* which, at least since Martinet, has been restricted to inflectional affixes.

In the most recent theory, morpheme is sometimes equated with the rules by which particular meanings determine the shape of word-forms (Anderson), or equated to a correlation between semantic similarity and phonological similarity (Bybee). It is these scholars, among others, who deny the validity of morphemes as theoretical constructs.

While it is impossible to give any definition which encompasses all of these various concepts, perhaps we can define a morpheme relatively uncontroversially as 'a set of **signs** whose members are synonymous and in complementary distribution', while adding to that definition (i) that a set may contain only one member, (ii) that in the most clear-cut instances, members of the set are clearly phonologically related to each other, and (iii) that the conditioning factor(s) for the complementary distribution can be stated in phonological rather than in lexical terms. Thus the plural endings on *cows* /kaʊz/, *horses* /hɔːsɪz/ and *cats* /kæts/ clearly resemble each other (in sharing a sibilant fricative) and are conditioned by the last sound in the **base**, and clearly meet the definition. However, if *oxen* and *children* and *alumni* are added to the list, the conditions are less clearly met. And while /waɪf/ and /waɪv/ (in *wife* and *wives*) are clearly phonologically similar, /beə/ and /bɜː/ (in *bear* and *birth*) are less obviously so, but there is no well-defined cut-off point on the scale of phonological relatedness.

The notation for marking morphemes is to enclose them in braces, so the morpheme which is shared by *cows*, *horses* and *cats* would be {s} or {plural} (both types of nomenclature are found) and /s/, /z/ and /ɪz/ are the allomorphs of that morpheme. (If the extension to cover *oxen*, *children* and *alumni* is allowed, /ən/, vowel-change +/rən/ and /aɪ/ are also allomorphs of the same morpheme.)

morpheme alternant is another label for **allomorph**.

morpheme structure condition A morpheme structure condition or MSC is a general statement about the phonological structure of morphemes in a given language. For example, in English it is an MSC that any nasal immediately preceding a final plosive in a morpheme should be homorganic with that plosive (*stand*, *camp*; **stamd*, **canp* are not possible English morphemes; in *harmed* the /m/ and the /d/ are not in the same morpheme).

morphological process A morphological process is any means of manipulating the form of a word for morphological purposes. **Compounding, affixation, back-formation, conversion** and so on are all morphological processes, despite their very different ways of building meaning in words.

morphological typology is the study of cross-linguistic patterns in the ways in which words are made up, paying no attention to aspects of word-structure derived from genetic inheritance. The usual typology of languages into **isolating, agglutinating, fusional** and **polysynthetic** goes back to the work of Wilhelm von Humboldt in the early nineteenth century, but seems to afford little predictive power.

morphologisation is a type of **grammaticalisation**. In morphologisation, what was originally a separate word becomes an element with a word. For example, the -*ric* in *bishopric* was originally a separate word, related historically to the German word *Reich* 'empire'.

morphome /ˈmɔːfəʊm/ A morphome is a cluster of signs which are in complementary distribution, and thus may mean the same as **morpheme** in one of its many uses. For example, -*s* as in *cats*, -*en* as in *oxen*, ablaut as in *feet*, -*im* as in *cherubim*, the replacement of -*us* by -*i* as in *cacti* are all members of the English morpheme which is used to mark plurality. However, while the meaning is important for the identification of a morpheme, it is not for the morphome. Thus the -*s* which marks adverbs in words like *besides*, *nights*, *overseas* may be a member of the same morphome as the -*s* which marks the third-person singular of the present tense in *deems*, *goes*, *instils*, even though these are two different morphemes.

The morphome used to mark plurality would be different, though, because it has more options within it. The notion was devised by Aronoff (1994).

morphophonemics /ˌmɔːfəʊfə'niːmɪks/ is the study of morphophonemes. Morphophonemes are positions in the phonological structure of a **morpheme** where different phonemes arise in different **allomorphs** of that morpheme. Consider the words *malign* and *malignant*, /məlaɪn/ and /məlɪgnənt/. If we consider that *malignant* is made up of two morphs, the second being *-ant*, then we find that we have two allomorphs of the morpheme {malign}: /məlaɪn/ and /məlɪgn/. Most phonologists analyse the difference as involving changes: /aɪ/ alternates with /ɪ/ and /g/ alternates with Ø (zero). The morphophoneme is the set of phonemes which alternate in one position. Thus /aɪ/ ~ /ɪ/ (where the swung dash indicates 'alternates with') is one morphophoneme of English which arises in several different morphemes (*divine, divinity; mine, mineral; sign, signal;* and so on). Morphophonemics, sometimes called 'morphophonology' or, less frequently, 'morphonology', deals with ways of describing this situation in grammars. Fundamental questions in morphophonemics include whether there is a basic underlying form of morphophonemes or not, and if so what restrictions there are on its form (see **underlier**); how distant from their surface phonemic representations morphophonemic representations are allowed to be; whether morphophonemic alternations are mental realities for speakers; and how morphophonemic alternations are tied to particular affixes or morphological processes (see **level-ordering**). A transcription which marks morphophonemes in some way or which uses underlying forms of morphemes is called a 'morphophonemic transcription', and is usually

enclosed within vertical bars (e.g. |mælıgn|), or some-
times within double verticals (e.g. ||mælıgn||) or braces
(e.g. {mælıgn}).

morphophonology or **morphonology** see **morphophonemics**

morphosyntactic word see **grammatical word** (1) and
grammatical word (2)

morphosyntax is that part of syntax for which morphology
is relevant, such as the definition of word-classes like
noun and verb, or the specification of **categories** such as
Tense and Number. A 'morphosyntactic feature' is one
which specifies a value for a morphosyntactic **property**
(e.g. [+ past]) which is morphological but required by the
syntax.

morphotactics is the (study of the) way in which morphs
are concatenated into words. There are several theories
about the way in which morphotactics is regulated:
(i) various morphological processes derive words of one
word-class from words of another, but apart from the
constraints that this implies, the sequencing of morphs
is essentially free; (ii) each morph carries with it a
specification of the morphs to which it may be adjacent
(or a specification that it closes a word and cannot have
further morphs added to it); (iii) morphemes fall into
classes whose morphological ordering and phonological
behaviour are distinct, and apart from the ordering of
the classes, ordering occurs as in (i); (iv) the order in
which the morphs can occur with any given stem is
determined by general principles of syntactic or semantic structure, the ordering being determined extra-
morphologically; (v) the order in which the morphs
can occur with any given stem is determined language-

specifically in terms of a template which provides a number of slots for morphs and specifies the classes of morph which may occur in each slot. See also **affix-ordering**.

MSC see **morpheme structure condition**

N

Natural Morphology is a theory of morphology which attempts to relate the facts of morphology back to universal semiotic or cognitive principles. Such principles may include facts about human perception. Thus perceptual ease makes **transparent** affixes, such as are found in *fit–fit·ted* and *sigh–sigh·ed*, easier to understand than the less transparent marking in *sit–sat* and *buy–bought*. **Constructional iconicity** is another type of principle of Natural Morphology. Natural Morphology has been developed especially in Austria and Germany by people like Wolfgang Dressler, Willi Mayerthaler and Wolfgang Wurzel. See also **naturalness**.

naturalness Being natural is the converse of being **marked** (2). A particular morphological phenomenon is natural if (i) it is widespread in the languages of the world, (ii) it arises frequently through language change, (iii) once it has arisen, it is itself resistant to language change, (iv) it is acquired early by children, (v) it is resistant to loss in aphasias, (vi) it arises early in the process of creolisation and (vii) it is common in the languages in which it occurs.

neo-classical compound Words like *photograph*, *telephone* or *genocide* are neo-classical compounds. They are made up of stems from the Classical languages, Latin and

Greek, but the words are constructed in modern times, and were never part of the Classical languages. The individual elements such as *photo-*, *tele-* and *-cide* are referred to as **combining forms**: *photo-* and *tele-* are initial combining forms, *-cide* is a final combining form. Combining forms may also be used in connection with independent words as in *teletransportation* and *insecticide*.

neologism /niːˈɒlədʒɪzm/ A neologism is a newly coined word. There is a tradition of restricting the term 'neologism' to a number of specific subsets of newly coined words: (i) where the word is coined by an experimenter to test reactions in a psychological or psycholinguistic experiment; (ii) where the newly coined word enters the general vocabulary of the language. Type (ii) is then contrasted with **nonce word**.

neuter see **gender**

no phrase constraint This postulated constraint says that because the morphological component of a language has input into the syntax but does not depend upon the syntax, there can be no phrases internally in words. Lexical items such as *forget-me-not*, which are lexicalised phrases, are probably not exceptions to this constraint, and there is dispute as to whether things like *an I-give-up shrug* or *the no phrase constraint* constitute genuine exceptions or not, because it is not clear whether the phrase is really internal in words. A noun such as *an I'm-right-ist*, where a suffix is added directly to the phrase, does break the constraint, though.

nominalisation is the formation of nouns by a morphological process, or a word which is the result of such a process.

Thus the formation of *bereavement* by suffixation from *bereave* is a process of nominalisation, and *bereavement* is itself a nominalisation.

Various types of nominalisation may be distinguished. 'Action nominalisations', sometimes sub-classified as 'act', 'fact', 'result', 'state' nominalisations (and possibly a few other labels) are forms such as *examination*, while 'subject nominalisations' or 'agent(ive) nominalisations' include forms such as *killer*.

nominative /'nɒmɪnətɪv/ see **case**

nonce word or **nonce-formation** /'nɒns ˌwɜːd/ A nonce word is a newly coined word, invented on the spot to serve some immediate need. For some authorities a nonce word is by definition ephemeral, and then contrasts with a **neologism**. Other authorities do not see any distinction between the two.

non-concatenative morphology is any kind of morphology which does not add sequential fixed-form morphs to each other to construct words. See also **ablaut, apophony, internal modification, reduplication, root-and-pattern, synaffix, umlaut.**

non-finite A non-finite verb is unrestricted in the temporal period that it can refer to, and is thus generally untensed. More generally, a non-finite verb cannot stand alone as the main verb in a sentence.

non-past see **tense**

notational conventions For various notational conventions see **boundary, gloss, lexeme, morph, morpheme, morphophonemics, word-form, zero morph.**

noun class A noun class is one member of a set of classes, usually based on form, into which the nouns of a particular language can be divided. Noun classes are usually relevant for agreement. Typically, different noun classes will show different markers for particular inflectional properties. The terms 'noun class' and **gender** are sometimes used interchangeably.

number is a morphological category, usually marked on the noun or pronoun, but also shown by agreement with verbs, adjectives and determiners, which shows how many entities are perceived as being involved. Simple number systems like that of modern English work with a division between singular (a single entity) and plural (more than one entity). More complex number systems may have a category of dual (referring to precisely two entities) or trial (referring to precisely three entities). Other systems may have a paucal category (referring to just a few entities). Other languages have a number system which reflects the way entities are usually discovered in the world. Nouns are unmarked for number when they refer to entities occurring in expected quantities, for example many ants, one nose. However, to refer to just one ant, the singulative is used, while to refer to many noses, the plurative is used. For other complexities of number see Corbett (2000).

O

oblique /ɔˈbliːk/ see **case**

once-only rule This term implies a certain view of the way in which word-formation rules work. According to the relevant theories, a new lexeme is created only once, and after that is retained in memory, so that it neither has to be created nor analysed by the user any more. The rules which create the word thus function only once. This notion is in conflict with views which hold that we understand complex words by analysing them.

opacity see **transparency** (1)

operand In **word-and-paradigm** morphology, the **base** to which structure-building rules apply is termed the 'operand'.

orthographic word see **word**

overgenerating morphology An overgenerating morphology is a morphological component of a grammar which allows for words to be created even though they are not established in the community whose language is being described. This means that a word like *goer* can be generated, although the word *goer* is not used to refer to just anyone who goes; nevertheless, an expression like *theatre-goer* seems to presuppose such a possibility.

P

Panini's principle see **elsewhere principle**

paradigm /ˈpærədaɪm/ The general meaning of paradigm is a set of forms (usually having something in common) which contrast with each other and can replace each other in a given context. Thus *me, you, him, her, it, us, them* form a paradigm of pronouns that can appear in a context such as *I saw* ___. More generally still, *moon* and *problem* can be said to be in a paradigmatic relationship with each other in that either could occur in *I saw the* ___.

More specifically, a paradigm is a set of **word-forms** realising the same **lexeme**. In the teaching of languages, such paradigms (the term derives from a Greek word meaning 'pattern' or 'model') are set out as learning tools so that students will be able to generalise from them to other words of the same **inflectional class**. Each position in the matrix can be termed a 'cell'. For example, the paradigm for a Latin noun (as a representative of a larger class of nouns) is given below:

DOMINUS 'lord'	Singular	Plural
Nominative	dominus	dominī
Vocative	dominē	dominī
Accusative	dominum	dominōs
Genitive	dominī	dominōrum
Dative	dominō	dominīs
Ablative	dominō	dominīs

'Paradigm' is sometimes used in a narrower sense, for example, *the paradigm of the singular of DOMINUS*, and sometimes in a wider sense, for example *the Latin nominal paradigm* (where the pattern of cells common to all inflection classes is meant).

The term 'paradigm' is also used for a set of derivationally related words which share a base (see **word-family**). So *aggress, aggression, aggressive, aggressively, aggressiveness, aggressor* or *baptise, baptist, baptistery, baptism, baptismal* may be termed 'derivational paradigms'. This use is considerably rarer than the inflectional one.

Paradigm Economy Principle For the sake of argument, assume that there is a language, a bit like German, which has four cases and several different declensions (see **inflection class**). We might find that no nominatives ever take an ending, that accusatives sometimes have no ending and sometimes take *-en*, that genitives sometimes take *-s* and sometimes take *-en* and sometimes *-e*, and that datives sometimes take *-en* , sometimes *-m*. It might seem logical that any relevant word would have a random pattern of endings associated with it, so that there would, in this fictitious instance, be twelve different possible declensions. The Paradigm Economy Principle, formulated by Andrew Carstairs-McCarthy, says that since in this example the maximum number of forms for any case is three, there will be no more than three different declensions. In other words, paradigms order the available material in such a way that memory load is minimised.

parasynthesis see **synaffix**

participle /'pɑːtɪsɪpəl/ In Latin grammatical terminology, a participle is a word which participates as both a verb (by showing **tense**) and as an adjective (by showing adjectival inflection). In modern usage, the term refers to a non-finite part of the verb other than the infinitive (independent of the function of these forms in the sentence). The forms of EXHAUST in (1) and (2) are the present and past participles respectively.

(1) a. The exhausting day was drawing to a close.
    b. The heat is exhausting me.
(2) a. The exhausted runner staggered past the finishing line.
    b. I have exhausted all possibilities.

A present participle used as a noun is called a 'gerund', for example *running* in *Running had worn me out*. In Latin grammar, the term 'gerundive' is used of a future passive participle used as an adjective, as *delenda* in *Delenda est Carthago* 'Carthage is fit.to.be.destroyed'. (A passive participle is a participle with a passive reading.) 'Gerundive' is used less specifically in describing other languages.

A noun with the form of a passive participle is called a 'supine' in Latin grammar.

partitive see **case**

passive see **voice**

past see **tense**

past participle see **participle**

paucal /ˈpɔːkəl/ see **number**

percolation or **feature percolation** describes the way in which information about the **heads** of structures is shared by the structure as a whole. This is usually envisaged as the copying of features from the node in the tree dominating the head of the construction to the node in the tree that dominates the entire construction. Precisely what information percolates up a tree in this manner is not clear, but it includes information about word-class and, where relevant, gender and inflection class.

perfect see **aspect**

perfective see **aspect**

person is a morphological category which distinguishes the speaker from the addressee and from other individuals discussed. The first person refers to the speaker ('I') or to a group including the speaker (e.g. 'we'). The second person refers to the individual or group of individuals addressed directly (so corresponding to 'you'). The third person is used of other individuals to whom reference is made (and so corresponds to meanings such as 'he, she, it, they'). Some languages also have a so-called fourth person to mention entities which are not already a focus in the current sentence. Although person is clearly a category of pronouns, it may also be marked on verbs, so that *walks* is the third-person-singular (present-tense) form of the English verb WALK.

petrified see **institutionalisation**

phonaestheme /ˈfəʊnəsθiːm/ A phonaestheme is a sequence of sounds which, while it often correlates with a particular meaning, cannot be analysed as a morph in a word because morphs lead to an exhaustive analysis of the word but phonaesthemes do not. The *gl-* in words like *gleam*, *glimmer*, *glitter* is often cited as a phonaestheme whose meaning can be glossed as 'having to do with light', and the *-ump* in words like *bump*, *thump* might mean 'making a dull sound'. Note that the meaning of phonaesthemes is often difficult to pin down precisely, and it may not be clear which words contain the relevant item: *glimpse* and *glory*, for example, may or may not contain the *gl-* element mentioned above. In any case, *-eam*, *-immer*, *-itter* and so on are not meaningful elements in *gleam*, *glimmer*, *glitter* and so on.

phonetic motivation is the impulse provided by phonetic form in the creation of a new word. See **ablaut-motivated compounding**, **phonaestheme**, **rhyme-motivated compounding**, **sound symbolism**.

phonological word see **word**

phrasal lexeme A phrasal lexeme is a **lexical item** made up of more than one word. The term is no longer considered appropriate because it implies that all lexemes are lexical items.

playful formation A playful formation is a word created for its superficial appeal rather than because its elements combine to give a serious meaning. Playful formations are particularly common in headlines, such as the one that was used when a dog was first sent up in a satellite (or sputnik): *Every dog-nik has its day-nik*. The *-nik* element is not meaningful, but brings *sputnik* to mind.

plural see **number**

plurative /'pluǝrǝtɪv/ see **number**

polysynthetic A polysynthetic language is a synthetic language in which the proportion of obligatorily bound morphs in the lexicon is unusually high, with the result that nouns and adverbials may be encoded by obligatorily bound morphs in words inflecting as verbs. Many North American languages, including languages such as Tlingit and Inuit, are cited as good examples of this type. Polysynthesis is not really a single phenomenon, but involves a number of subsidiary features, not all of which will necessarily be present in any given language. One of the most important of these is the use of **incorporation**. English does not have any real polysynthetic morphology, but comes close to incorporation in a verb like *baby-sit*. See also **agglutinating, fusional, isolating**.

popular etymology see **folk etymology**

portmanteau morph This term has two closely related meanings. (1) A word in which two expected words can be seen to be conflated, for example French *du* 'of the' rather than **de le*. (2) Any **morph** which through **cumulation** realises more than one morphosyntactic **property**, for example the final *-o* in Italian *zio* 'uncle', which shows the word to be both masculine and singular.

portmanteau word see **blend**

positional mobility is one of the criteria for internal cohesion in the definition of the **grammatical word** (2). It means that a word can occur in different places in a sentence, as *unfortunately* in *Unfortunately he is ill* and *He is unfortunately ill*.

possessive usually means the same as 'genitive', see **case**.

possible word or **potential word** A potential word is one which is not attested but which is expected to be possible given the state of the language system. While *bibliography* is an **actual word** of English, *biblographise* is not, but could be coined and used if it were needed. As such, it is a potential word of English at the present time. A potential word is well formed and grammatical but not attested.

potentiation The addition of a particular affix is said to 'potentiate' the addition of some other affix when it makes the addition of the second affix possible. In simple cases this is a matter of word-class: the suffix *-ise* potentiates the addition of *-s*, *-ed* and *-ing* because these suffixes are added to verbs, and *-ise* creates verbs. In other cases potentiation is more subtle. For example, the addition of *-ise* potentiates *-ation* rather than *-ment*, whereas the prefixation of *en-* to a verb in some patterns potentiates *-ment* (as in *ennoblement*).

pre-emption see **blocking**

prefix A prefix is an **affix** added before its **base**. In *unhelpful*, *un-* is a prefix.

prefixation is the addition of a **prefix** to a base.

present see **tense**

present participle see **participle**

preterite /ˈprɛtərɪt/ is a past **tense**.

primary compound see **compound**

process see **morphological process**

proclitic see **clitic**

productivity deals with the extent to which new words may be coined by any particular morphological process. Productivity may be broken down into two subsidiary parts. *Disponibilité* (the term is from Danielle Corbin and is translated into English as 'availability') is a matter of whether a particular process may be used at all in the production of new words. A process is either available or unavailable. One that is available is sometimes said to be 'living'. *Rentabilité* (translated into English as 'profitability') looks at available processes and asks how much they are used. Various measures of profitability have been suggested in the literature, though there are problems with all of them. Either type of productivity is usually seen as being a phenomenon which affects a language community rather than an individual, so that certain individuals may continue to coin words using a particular process even when that process is no longer generally available to the community. Profitability is sometimes taken to be a phenomenon which is best considered in particular domains. For example, the suffixation of *-ation* to a verb to create a noun is probably 100 per cent profitable on verbs which end in *-ise*, but may not even be available on verbs ending in *-en*.

profitability see **productivity**

progressive see **aspect**

proper inclusion principle see **elsewhere principle**

property, morphosyntactic A 'morphosyntactic' or 'morphological property' is a term used within **word-and-paradigm** morphology to refer to the features for which a particular word may be inflected. For example, Latin nouns may be inflected, among other things, for properties such as nominative, accusative, ablative which are morphosyntactic properties belonging to the morphosyntactic **category** of Case.

R

realisation is the relationship between concrete elements such as **morphs** and **word-forms** and their corresponding abstract constructs, **morphemes** and **lexemes**. Morphs 'realise' or 'make real' abstract morphemes because morphs have actual phonological shape or form, while morphemes are the constructs of the analyst. See also **exponence**.

reanalysis occurs when speakers fail to perceive the original morphological structure of a word and interpret it as though it has some other structure. The reanalysis of an earlier singular form *pease* (now remembered mainly in the expression *pease pudding*) as *pea+s* led to the formation of a singular form *pea* in the history of English. An earlier English form *a naperon* was also reanalysed to give modern English *an apron*. **Folk etymology** is another type of reanalysis.

reciprocal is the term used to describe a morphological property which indicates that the participants in an action carry out the action on each other. In the Danish farewell *vi se·s* 'we see·'S'', the final *-s* has reciprocal force since it indicates that all of the participants will see all of the others.

rection is an old term for **government**.

redundancy rule A redundancy rule states a relationship between items without any implication that one derives from the other or is logically prior to the other. Some scholars believe that unproductive **morphophonemic** rules such as that between /aɪ/ and /ɪ/ in *malign* and *malignant* are best stated as redundancy rules. Others believe that many derivatives are related to their bases only through redundancy rules, which simply state, for example, that words of the form X and Xness (where X represents any adjective) are possibly related to each other. The implication is that speakers do not form Xness on the basis of X, but can relate the two if they happen to know both words.

reduplicant /rɪˈdjuːplɪkənt/ The reduplicant is the part of a reduplicated word which is not the base. In Motu, a language of Papua New Guinea, the plural of *mero* 'boy' is *memero*, and the first *me-* is the reduplicant. See also **reduplication**.

reduplication is the repetition of some part of the **base** (possibly all of the base) as a **morphological process**. When disyllabic verbs take a plural subject in Samoan, one common way of showing this is to reduplicate the first consonant and vowel of the base, so *nofo* 'sit' gives *nonofo* in the plural, while *moe* 'sleep' gives *momoe* and *fasi* 'to beat' gives *fafasi*. In other languages, it may be the last part of a word which is reduplicated, with the **reduplicant** suffixed to the base.

reflexive is the term used to describe a morphological property which indicates that the participants in an action carry out the process on themselves. In French *se raser*, 'to shave' the *se* indicates that the action is reflexive.

relevance is a principle introduced by Joan Bybee to explain **affix-ordering** cross-linguistically. Affixes marking more relevant categories are found closer to the root than affixes marking less relevant categories, other things being equal. Relevance is defined as the semantic effect that a particular category has on the base to which it is attached. For example, aspect, which says something about the internal make-up of an event, is more relevant to a verb than tense, which says something about the time at which the event occurred. Accordingly, aspect is usually marked closer to the verbal root than tense in languages which mark both. Also, aspectual difference is more likely to lead to the creation of new lexemes than is tense difference. On nouns, gender is more relevant than number, so that the ordering found in *lion·ess·es* is expected, and the fact that gender sometimes is marked in a different lexeme (e.g. *mare*, *ewe*, *woman*) is expected. See also **lexical generality**.

rendaku /rɛnˈdækuː/ is a **morphophonemic** process in some Japanese compounds whereby an initial voiceless consonant becomes voiced in the compound structure. For example, the word *amadera* 'nunnery' is made up of the words *ama* 'nun' and *tera* 'temple'.

rentabilité see **productivity**

repeated morph constraint This postulated constraint states that an affix can never be repeated adjacent to itself within a word. Thus, while *murder·er* is a perfectly good word of English when the first -*er* is not a morph, *kill·er·er* could never be a permissible word. In might be possible to have the same affix twice in a word if the repetitions are not adjacent: *contain·er·is·er*, for example, might be a possible word of English.

As stated this constraint is too strong, since German *Ur·ur·gross·vater* 'great·great·grand·father' is quite normal, and we occasionally find words in English like *meta-meta-file*. Such examples are, however, rare, and tend to be semantically coherent, with each repetition of the affix denoting a new cycle of some event.

Occasionally this constraint may give rise to questions concerning what counts as the same affix. For example, *He talked to her in a fatherly manner* is fine, but **He talked to her fatherlily* is not. Does **fatherlily* run foul of the repeated morph constraint or is there some other reason for its impossibility? There is some suggestion that the repeated morph constraint might be largely a phonological constraint, since, for example, modern English speakers tend to avoid *sillily*, which has a repeated syllable but not a repeated morph. Forms like *murderer* seem to argue against this position.

replacive morph The term 'replacive morph' indicates a now out-dated view of **ablaut**. At one time the relationship between *run* and *ran* was said to involve a replacive morph: *-a-* replaces the *-u-* in the past tense. This was a way of smuggling processes into **item and arrangement** descriptions. Note that a replacive morph is not a form, though a **morph** is generally a form.

reversative is the term used to describe a morphological process which creates a word whose meaning indicates a reversal of the action of the base. It may also label a word formed by such a process. English *undo* is a reversative.

rhyme-motivated compounding refers to the juxtaposition of word-like elements which are related to each other by rhyme. Words like *hokey-pokey* and *teeny-weeny* illustrate the phenomenon. These words are sometimes called 'echo words'. Note that these are not really compounds, since they are not necessarily made up of two independent words, though we also find rhyme supporting the formation of more ordinary compounds such as *brain-drain* and *gang-bang*. See also **ablaut-motivated compounding**.

right-hand head rule This so-called rule is no more than a tendency for the **head** of a word to be the right-most morph in that word. Many languages have left-headed compounds, for example French *bateau-mouche* 'boat-fly', which is a kind of boat, and English has some derivatives whose word-class is determined by the prefix, which must accordingly be the head: [en[circle]ₙ]ᵥ. The tendency to right-headedness is sufficiently widespread to be rule-like in some languages such as Dutch, and is felt strongly in others such as English, but many languages do not have a consistent ordering of head and modifier in morphology.

root A root is the smallest unanalysable **base**, or what remains after all **affixes** have been removed from a word. In *unfriendliness*, the root is *friend*; in French *donnerions* 'we would give' the root is *donn-*.

root-and-pattern Root-and-pattern or **introflection** are labels used to refer to the complex pattern of **internal modification** found mainly in Semitic and Berber languages. 'Introflection' is used especially by typologists, 'root-and-pattern' mainly within **Auto-segmental Morphology**. In these languages, the **root** in a number of common **binyanim** or **paradigms** may be analysed as being made up solely of consonants, while the pattern of the vowels which are found around the consonants and the particular vowels filling up the pattern provide morphological information comparable to that often given by affixation. This analysis leads to discontinuous roots and discontinuous morphs inter-acting with the roots, both of which are marked struc-tures. Alternative explanations are sought in a number of models of morphology. See also **apophony, transfix**.

root compound see **compound**

[S]

second person see **person**

semi-productivity is sometimes taken to be a defining feature of derivational morphology. If a morphological process is semi-productive, it is available (see **productivity**), but still cannot be used freely. Thus while we can find *-ette* in words like *usherette* and *majorette*, it may still not be acceptable in, say, *bettorette*.

separation hypothesis The separation hypothesis, associated particularly with the name of Robert Beard, is the hypothesis that the function of a morphological process is autonomous of the processes which spell out or identify the actual morphs used to realise that function in individual instances. Thus there is a function of nominalisation in English which affects verbs like *endow*, *exert*, *laugh*, *organise*, *renew*, *tumble*, but in each case the process used to create the nominalised verb is different, as in *endowment*, *exertion*, *laughter*, *organisation*, *renewal*, *tumble* (note the instance of conversion in the last case). At the same time, the same marker may have different functions, as with the final *-s* in *cars*, *ducks* (as a term of address), *expects*, *preggers*, *towards*. Keeping the meaning and the form separate from each other avoids many of the problems of synonymy and polysemy that arise from treating each nominalisation process, for example, as a different synonymous process, or from treating the various *-s* affixes as variants of a single form.

sign A sign, in Saussurean linguistics, is a linguistic element which has both a form (a *signifiant* or *signifier*) and a meaning (the *signifié* or *signified*). A morpheme like {tree} which only ever has one form can be seen as a sign.

simple see **simplex**

simple clitic see **clitic**

simplex contrasts with **complex** and is used to denote a word
which is **monomorphemic,** that is, is made up of a single
morpheme with no morphological structure. 'Simple' is
sometimes used with the same meaning.

simulfix is a rarely used term for **superfix.**

singular see **number**

singulative /ˈsɪŋgjʊlətɪv/ see **number**

slot A slot is either (1) a position in a **template** or (2),
informally, a **cell** in a **paradigm.**

sound symbolism is the use of sound structure to reflect
semantic structure in an iconic way. For example, in
many languages deictics which show closeness to the
speaker have a closer vowel than deictics which show
distance from the speaker: *this* versus *that* in English, *ici*
'here' versus *là* 'there' in French. The closeness of the
tongue to the roof of the mouth is supposed to reflect
iconically the closeness of the relationship. Similarly, it is
often claimed that **diminutives** have closer vowels and/or
more palatal consonants than **augmentatives,** although
such a relationship does not hold in all languages.

special clitic see **clitic**

spell out is the set of processes in a **separationist** model
(including **distributed morphology**) which specify the
phonological form of a morph in a given environment.

splinter A splinter is a fraction of a word, arising in a **blend,**

then used as an affix to create more words, as *-nomics* in *Reaganomics, Clintonomics, Thatchernomics* and so on.

split morphology is the name given to the theory that inflectional and derivational morphology are of essentially different types, and cannot be dealt with in the same component.

stative see **aspect**

stem (1) In British usage, a stem is the **base** for any **inflectional** process. Thus in the construction of French *donn·er·ai* 'I shall give' *donn-* is the stem for the suffixation of *-er*, and *donner-* is the stem for the suffixation of *-ai*. Some lexemes may have more than one stem. Thus the German verb STEHEN 'to stand' has at least the two stems *steh-* and *stand-* found in, for example, the forms *stehen* and *standen*.

stem (2) Within lexicalist theories of morphology, a stem is an obligatorily bound **base**, usually in a **derivational** process. Thus in the word *botanic*, the stem is *botan-*, which cannot stand alone as a word, and the suffix is *-ic*. The term '(obligatorily) bound base' is also in use, but is more unwieldy.

stem-based morphology describes the situation when the affixes in a **paradigm** are added to something which cannot stand alone as a word. Latin is a typical example of a language which has stem-based morphology: the stem in *dominus* is *domin-* which cannot occur without some final affix. See also **word-based morphology**.

stem extender A stem extender is a formal element which is added to a **stem** (1) before inflectional affixes are added.

An alternative analysis always exists whereby the stem extender creates a new allomorph of the stem. One of the best-known stem extenders is the **thematic vowel** found in the verbs in many Romance languages.

subject nominalisation see **nominalisation**

subjunctive see **mood**

subtraction is the removal of material from a word as a morphological process. While material is removed from words in **clipping**, this may not be a morphological process. However, the derivation of French masculine adjectives from the corresponding feminine adjectives, while counterintuitive for most French speakers, shows a neat pattern which corresponds to a morphological distinction. If we consider the masculine and feminine forms of some French adjectives in their spoken form, we find examples like the following: /blã, blãʃ/ 'white', /fʁwa, fʁwad/ 'cold', /gʁo, gʁos/ 'large', /pəti, pətit/ 'small'. From the masculine form it is impossible to predict what the final consonant in the feminine form will be, but from the feminine form it is always possible to predict the masculine: delete the final consonant. Thus an analysis which works by subtraction has a logical basis. Such instances are rare, and speakers often seem to use less efficient ways of representing mentally the relationship between the pairs.

suffix A suffix is an **affix** attached after its **base**. In *fatherly*, *-ly* is a suffix.

suffixation is the addition of a **suffix** to a **base**.

suffixing preference There are many languages which use suffixes but not prefixes, and very few languages where prefixes are used but not suffixes. In languages which have both, suffixes tend to be more common than prefixes. Thus cross-linguistically there is a preference for suffixes over not only prefixes but also over all other kinds of affixes, and this is called the 'suffixing preference'.

superfix or **suprafix** are now little-used names for some types of **internal modification**. Where a morphological change is marked by a change in the suprasegmental structure of the base (rather than by affixation, etc.), this was called a 'superfix', on the grounds that the suprasegmentals represented a type of **affix** which overlay the 'real' segmental structure of the base. For instance, the difference in stress in the English noun–verb pairs *'import–im'port*, *'transfer–trans'fer* is referred to by some scholars as a superfix. The terms are used less these days as such changes are no longer viewed as affixation.

superlative /suːˈpɜːlətɪv/ see **comparison**

suppletion /səˈpliːʃən/ is the name given to the situation where etymologically unrelated forms are used in the paradigm of the same lexeme. For example, *went*, now the past tense of GO, was once a form of WEND. Many scholars recognise various degrees of suppletion, including unpredictable but related forms as instances of suppletion and extending the notion to derivational paradigms. While everyone would accept *am* and *be* as instances of suppletion, some would also include *Glasgow* and *Glasweg·ian* as showing suppletion.

suprafix see **superfix**

synaffix /'sınəfıks/ A synaffix is another way of accounting for the phenomenon known as 'parasynthesis', namely the appearance of more than one affix simultaneously to mark a particular meaning. The best-known synaffix is the **circumfix**, where material is simultaneously prefixed and suffixed, but there are also instances where, for example, prefixed and infixed material go together to show a particular meaning, or internal modification and affixation together show a particular meaning (as in English *stolen* from *steal*).

syncretism /'sıŋkrətızm/ A syncretism arises when words in two distinct cells in a **paradigm** have the same form, although other paradigms in the same language have different forms in the corresponding cells. For example, identity of form for the nominative and accusative singular of BELLUM 'war' in the set of Latin data shown below is a syncretism because the two equivalent forms are distinct in some declensions.

Latin singular nouns	'war'	'master'	'girl'
Nominative	bellum	dominus	puella
Accusative	bellum	dominum	puellam

syntax of words The syntax of words is an approach to morphology associated with Elisabeth Selkirk. In this model, the general principles of syntax are taken to apply at the morphological level as well as at the syntactic level, and affixes are lexical items which can be inserted into syntactic trees to give morphologically complex words. The notion of the **head** of a word is particularly important in the syntax of words model.

synthetic A synthetic construction is one which uses morphologically complex words rather than a sequence of simple words. Thus modern written French has a synthetic future in *je chanterai* 'I shall sing' while modern spoken French frequently prefers the **analytic** future *je vais chanter* 'I am going to sing'.

A synthetic language is one which shows a general preference for morphologically complex words, particularly for inflection. See also **agglutinating, fusional, polysynthetic**.

synthetic compound see **compound**

T

target In **agreement**, the target is the element whose form is determined by the **controller**. If adjectives agree with nouns for number and gender, for example, as in Romance and Bantu, the adjective is the target; the verb is the target of subject–verb agreement.

tatpuruṣa /tætpʊˈruːʃə/ is the name given by the Sanskrit grammarians to what are sometimes called determinative **compounds** in English. These are compounds in which there is a clear modifier–modified relationship within the compound. The modification is shown by hyponymy (a *whiteboard* is a kind of board, not a kind of white, but *white* says what kind of board).

telic /ˈtɛlɪk/ see **aspect**

templatic morphology see **affix-ordering, morphotactics**

tense is a morphological category (usually marked on the verb) which relates the time of the action denoted by the verb to some other time, usually to the moment of speaking. The most familiar tenses are the past, referring to things which have occurred before the moment of speaking, the present, referring to things which are ongoing at the time of speaking, and the future, referring to things which have not yet happened at the time of speaking. While English has a morphological present tense and a morphological past tense, though, it has no morphological future tense, and can use the so-called present tense to refer to future events (*His plane arrives later this evening*). For this reason, some prefer the label 'non-past' for this tense. Other languages may have tenses such as recent past or remote past (some languages may have five or more distinctions in terms of remoteness). Many other distinctions which are sometimes considered to be matters of tense are more properly viewed as distinctions of **aspect**.

termination is a now old-fashioned term for a suffix, especially an inflectional one.

thematic vowel A thematic vowel is one type of **stem extender** associated particularly with the Romance languages. In Italian, the first-person perfect of AMARE 'to love' is *amavo*, while the equivalent form of the verb TEMERE 'to fear' is *temevo*. The roots are respectively *am-* and *tem-*, and the perfect affix is the *-v-*. The intervening *-a-* or *-e-* shows the conjugation of the verb, but carries no meaning (see **inflection class**). It is an **empty morph**, 'morphological glue' holding the root to the affixes. Because it can be seen as creating a **stem** (1) from a **root**, it is called a thematic vowel (from **theme**).

theme is a now rather out-dated term for **stem** (1).

third person see **person**

token frequency The token frequency of a particular affix is calculated from the number of times that affix appears in a text, whatever base it is attached to. Thus if the affix is *-ism* and the word *cannibalism* appears twice, this will add two to the tokens of *-ism*. Lack of productivity of an affix is said to lead to a high token frequency of that affix, but a low **type frequency**.

transfix A transfix is a particular type of **affix**, one which is completely interwoven with its base. Typically, it is a series of vowels which surround and interact with a base which in turn can be analysed as a series of consonants. For example, Arabic *katab* 'he wrote', *kitaab* 'book', *kaatib* 'clerk' (where the root is *ktb, indicating 'writing') illustrate the transfixes *_a_a_*, *_i_aa_* and *_aa_i_*. Such transfixes, found mainly in the Semitic and Berber languages, are discontinuous affixes attached to discontinuous bases, and as such are viewed as very marked or unnatural structures. Many scholars prefer to view such structures in terms of **apophony** or **internal modification** rather than as root and affix. See also **root-and-pattern**.

transitive A verb is transitive if it has a direct object, intransitive if it does not have one. Transitivity is sometimes applied to other word-classes, in particular to prepositions (intransitive prepositions being things like the *down* in *I looked down*, which other scholars view as adverbs). See also **ditransitive, intransitive**.

transitiviser A transitiviser is a morphological element which when added to an **intransitive** verb changes it to a **transitive** one.

translative see **case**

transparency (1) A morphologically complex word is transparent to the extent that the user of the word can see and analyse the **morphs** within the word. Transparency can become weaker (and eventually vanish) if the form of the morph is altered in the word (see **morphophonemics**) or if the meaning of the word is no longer clearly related to the meaning of the morph in isolation. Form-change is illustrated by *div[ɪz]ive* from *div[aɪd]*; meaning change is illustrated with *health*, originally related to *heal* and to *hale*. When the analysis of a word is no longer transparent, the elements in the word or their relations with their erstwhile allomorphs are said to become 'opaque'.

transparency (2) Affixes are transparent if they appear in a position where we might expect to find the **head** of a word, but they do not mark the word-class of the word as a whole. Instead the word takes its word-class from the root or from a less peripheral affix. The affix is transparent in the sense that the rules must 'see through' the affix to find the word-class elsewhere. In Italian, diminutive suffixes are transparent as can be seen in the examples below.

tavolo	'table'	tavolino	'little table'
giallo	'yellow'	giallino	'yellowish'
bene	'well'	benino	'so-so'

The word-class of the word as a whole is derived from the root rather than from the suffix, which is added to many word-classes without affecting them. This type of transparency may apply to properties other than word-class: for instance, some affixes may not determine the gender of the word they form, and can be said to be transparent to gender.

See also **class-changing** and **class-maintaining**.

transposition in Marchand's theory of word-formation is the use of a word in a function which it does not normally have, for example the use of a verb as a modifier to an adjective in *fail-safe*. More generally, transposition is understood as change of lexical class without any addition of semantic specification. In this reading, the *-al* which changes *parent* to *parental* causes transposition. See also **conversion**.

trial see **number**

truncation is a morphophonemic process which is assumed to delete material from a base before a particular affix is added. Thus *nominee* is usually assumed to be derived from *nominate*, but with the truncation of *-ate* before the addition of *-ee*.

type familiarity A word which a speaker has never previously met may nevertheless be type familiar if there are other known words constructed according to the same pattern. A speaker who knows *hardware* and *software* may not be familiar with the particular words *wetware* 'human who programs a computer' or *vapourware* 'software which is projected but never completed'; these last two are nevertheless type familiar. Type familiarity is considered to be a prerequisite for **productivity**. Compare **item familiarity**.

type frequency The type frequency of an affix in a given text is calculated from the number of different lexemes in which the affix occurs. Thus if the affix is *-ism* and the word *cannibalism* occurs twice in the text, it will add only one to the type frequency of *-ism*. Increased **productivity** is said to lead to a rise in the type frequency of the productive affix, though each type (or **lexeme**) will have a relatively low **token frequency**.

U

umlaut /ˈʊmlaʊt/ is a type of **internal modification** involving vowels. 'Umlaut' refers specifically to alternations between vowels which arose because of the effect of some following vowel sound. For instance, the relationship between *foot* and *feet* is one of umlaut. In older stages of English, the plural of *foot* had the same vowel in the stem of the singular and the plural, and a suffix including an /i/ vowel, and this influenced the vowel in the root to make it into a front vowel. Eventually the /i/ was lost, and only the changed vowel was left. In the writing of German, this historical relationship was indicated by writing first the letter *e* and later a dieresis over the affected vowel. This written mark (shown in the first vowel of *Väter* 'fathers') is also called an umlaut. The distinction between umlaut and **ablaut** is a matter of the history of the Germanic languages. Synchronically, both are types of **apophony**.

underlier An underlier is the single phonological representation of a morpheme in a **morphophonemic** theory which demands these.

uninterruptability is one of the criteria for internal cohesion in the definition of a **grammatical word** (2). It means that morphs from elsewhere in the sentence cannot freely move into a word, so that *Freedom is important* does not have a variant *Freeisdom important*.

unique morph A unique morph is a **morph** which occurs in only one word or expression in the language being considered. In English, examples of unique morphs which are often cited are *kith* in the phrase *kith and kin*, and *-ric* in *bishopric*. There are some other less clear cases, including the *cran-* in *cranberry*. Although this is etymologically related to the name of the bird *crane*, any semantic link has long since vanished. Accordingly, unique morphs are sometimes termed 'cranberry morphs'. 'Bilberry morph' would be a theoretically sounder name.

unitary base hypothesis According to the unitary base hypothesis, the **base** for any **morphological process** need never be stated as a disjunction (that is, as either A or B). Although originally intended as a restriction on possible base types, this can also be read as a restriction on polysemy of affixes: at the point where an affix can be added to either an adjective or a noun, we must be dealing with two homophonous affixes, not a single affix. Given various theories of word-classes, it is, in any case, not clear that adjective and noun could not be captured by a unitary statement (e.g. [+N]), and this may weaken the hypothesis.

unitary output hypothesis This hypothesis states that the output of a single morphological process is always constant: an affix cannot produce, for example, nouns in some places and verbs in others.

unmarked *Love* is unmarked in relation to *loved* because it does not carry the marker *-(e)d*. Unmarked terms tend to be more frequent than their corresponding marked terms, partly because they tend to have a wider distribution. There is a tendency for the same properties to be unmarked across languages. See also **marked**, **naturalness**.

V

valency /'veɪlənsi/ is concerned with the number of arguments a verb (or other type of word) can take, and the nature of those arguments, either semantically or in terms of **case**. See **ditransitive, intransitive, transitive.**

verbal compound see **compound**

verbalisation is the formation of verbs by a morphological process, or a word which is the result of such a process. Thus the formation of *hospitalise* by suffixation from *hospital* is a process of verbalisation, and *hospitalise* is itself a verbalisation.

verbal-nexus compound see **compound**

vocative /'vɒkətɪv/ see **case**

voice is a morphological category marked on the verb which allows changes of focus by making different arguments of the verb the subject of the verb. The sentence *The farmer killed the duckling* is in the active voice, and *the farmer* is the agent and the subject of the verb, while in the corresponding passive *The duckling was killed by the farmer*, the direct object of the active verb becomes the subject of the passive verb. Correspondingly, in ergative/absolutive languages (see **case**), the noun phrase in the ergative case in the active voice becomes an absolutive argument in the antipassive voice. A sentence such as *This shirt washes well* is said to show the middle voice, though 'middle voice' has slightly different meaning in other languages.

vowel mutation see **apophony, internal modification**

W

WFR see **word-formation rule**

word The word is the fundamental unit of **morphology**, and yet it is its least well-defined unit, and word and **morpheme** between them are the terms which have the most different uses. Some authorities have even stated overtly than no universal definition of the word is possible. Nevertheless, this is attempted here.

We can define a word as a constituent which is intermediate in structure between the morpheme and the syntactic phrase, and which has a certain psychological salience. While such a definition appears to be accurate, it does not necessarily allow a 'word' to be uniquely identified, and it says nothing at all about the origins or significance of the psychological salience.

The psychological salience can be seen in the fact that many languages have an expression meaning 'word' (even though the 'word' thus labelled may be of a very different nature in languages of different types), and that speakers of many languages can cite 'words' of their language. Sapir claimed that even illiterate speakers of unwritten languages have no difficulty with the notion of a word, and while this may have to be taken with a small pinch of salt given the trouble that semi-literate speakers of written languages sometimes have with the same notion, there seems to be some truth to it – even if it is not true for all languages or all language types. This salience may, however, be derived from one or more of the factors discussed below.

There are a number of criteria at different levels of language which may conspire to identify a word in any particular language. We can separate some of these out.

An 'orthographic word' is a word as recognised by the

spelling system of a particular language. While there is no such entity in unwritten languages, and, indeed, no such entity in many written languages where words are not treated as orthographic elements, in languages with a long tradition of orthography, the orthographic word exerts a powerful influence on people's intuitions about the nature of a word. While due consideration has to be given to the status of punctuation marks, especially the hyphen and the apostrophe, in any firm definition of an orthographic word for a particular language, nevertheless most literate speakers of English, at least, seem to associate the term 'word' with an orthographic reality.

Many naïve speakers believe there to be 'phonetic words', separated off from each other by pauses (or, sometimes, potential pauses). In most conversation, however, there is no pause between words in the same syntactic unit, and there may be pauses in the middles of things which are otherwise considered to be words, so this notion has to be abandoned in this simple form.

There are, however, 'phonological words', words defined by the phonological systems of the individual language, though different criteria may be used to identify these in different languages (or, even, by different scholars in the same language). In those languages which have it, vowel harmony (the use within a word of vowels from specific sub-sets which match for some phonological feature such as frontness/backness) is often strongly correlated with word-hood, while in other languages stress may correlate with word-hood. In English the use of the stress criterion may lead to a 'word' like *correspondence* being seen as two phonological words (on the pattern of *funny sentence*).

'Morphological words' may be defined in a number of different ways. We can, for instance, see a morphological word being defined in terms of the paradigm in which the word appears. Thus we might say that the second-person singular of the present tense indicative of the Latin verb AMO, *amas*, is defined by the place in the verbal **paradigm** that it occupies. See **grammatical word (1)**. A morphological word might also be defined in terms of its **morphotactics**. Thus, we might want to say that any time we meet a past tense *-ed* in English we are at the end of a verb-word. This kind of definition appears to have some validity in languages like West Greenlandic, where a person/tense marker appears only once in the longest verb-word, and marks the end of that word. Where such an entity proves useful, we might call it a 'morphotactic word'.

A word may also be defined in terms of the syntax, again in a number of ways. It may be defined in terms of its internal coherence and external movability (see **grammatical word (2)**). It may be defined by its imperviousness to syntactically relevant processes such as reference (as within **lexicalist** theories of morphology). This makes it what has been termed a 'syntactic atom'. It may be defined by being the output of a block of rules which allow for lexical irregularities and the input to a set of syntactic rules which are fully productive (see **word-form**). It may be defined as an element whose variant forms occur in sentence-structure according to the demands of a set of syntactic requirements (see **lexeme**). Again other definitions are no doubt possible.

The semantics of a word and its lexical standing are intimately entwined. We might say that the distinction between a **function word** and a **content word** is one of semantics, while the semantic unity of a word defines an item as one which may have lexical status and so which is assumed to be listed as an element in the lexicon (see **lexical item**).

Whether there are other ways of defining words

independent of these aspects of their behaviour is an open question. Where several of these criteria coincide, it seems reasonable to use the ordinary-language term 'word'. Some morphologists prefer either to use 'word' to refer to just one of these many meanings, the one they feel is the default usage within their theory (e.g. Matthews), or to use it as a cover-term for all of these different views of the word, especially in instances where the precision of some of the terms suggested above may be spurious (e.g. Bauer).

word-and-paradigm Word-and-paradigm morphology, some-times abbreviated as WP, is the name given to the model of morphology deriving from ancient Greek and Roman views of language. The fundamental units in WP are the **word-forms**, each of which belongs to a **lexeme**. The form of the word-form is not derived from a sequence of morphs; rather the morphosyntactic features of the word demanded by the syntax are realised, together with the stem, as an unanalysable word-form. In WP, morphs and morphemes are not fundamental units, and it is no surprise if the word is not analysable into a sequence of morphs; so the *-us* on the end of Latin *dominus* is not in itself a unit and is not divisible into a 'nominative' marker and a 'singular' marker – rather *dominus* is 'the nominative singular of (the lexeme) DOMINUS', and while its phonological form is largely predictable from basic principles of the system, the links between form and meaning are not given any status in the theory. Word-and-paradigm morphology was formalised by Peter Matthews in the early 1970s, and eventually evolved into **a-morphous morphology**. See also **item and arrangement, item and process**.

word-based hypothesis The word-based hypothesis states

that the **base** in all derivational morphology is something that is a word (in the sense of **lexeme**). Thus the derivation of *fatherhood* from *father* fits with the word-based hypothesis, but a word like *ludic*, based on a Latin root meaning 'play' is probably not. In his original formulation of the word-based hypothesis Aronoff (1976: 21) also adds that the only words which can serve as bases in such derivations are nouns, verbs or adjectives. Words like *downer*, *thusly*, *uppity* suggest that this is too strong, even if it is generally true.

word-based morphology describes the situation when the affixes in a **paradigm** are added to something which can stand alone as a word. English is a typical example of a language which has word-based morphology: the stem in *dogs* is *dog*, which can occur without any final affix. See **stem-based morphology**.

word-family A word-family is a set of lexemes derived from the same base. *Father*, *fatherly*, *fatherhood*, *fatherland*, *godfather* are all members of the word-family based round *father*. The size of a word-family has been shown to influence the ease with which speakers can mentally access members of the family.

word-form is the technical term used for one of the meanings of **word**. In English we might want to say that *came*, *come*, *comes*, *coming* are all the same word, or we might want to say that they are all different words. In the sense in which they are different words, we use the term 'word-form'. Notationally, word-forms are marked by the use of italics, or underlining in manuscript (Lyons), so that we can say that *come* (along with *came*, *comes* and *coming*) is one of the forms of (the lexeme) COME. The literature is unclear on whether *banks* 'financial institutions' and *banks* 'tilts while turning' are the same word-from or homophonous word-forms, though the latter seems more defensible. See also **inflection, lexeme.**

word-formation There are several distinguishable meanings of word-formation. The most usual is that word-formation is the study of the creation of **lexemes** (see **lexeme-formation**). Word-formation may also be seen as the processes by which new lexemes are created, including **derivational** morphology, **compounding, conversion** and processes which are less obviously morphological, such as **blending, clipping,** the creation of **acronyms,** and the like. Some authorities include **inflectional** morphology under the general heading of word-formation, and so it may be the study of all morphology, or any morphological process.

word-formation rule A word-formation rule or WFR is a rule used in the construction of any word of complex structure. While word-formation rules are generally thought of as being rules of **compounding** or **derivational** morphology, they may, for some writers, include rules of **inflectional** morphology.

word manufacture is the creation of a new **lexeme** without any reference to constituent morphemes or, indeed, to anything except phonemic structure. Word manufacture is a rare process for the creation of ordinary lexemes, although a few slang terms may have been created this way, for instance *scag* 'heroin' and *boff* 'have sexual intercourse with'. The use of word manufacture is most obvious in the creation of trade-names. *Kodak* is perhaps the most famous example of this. The name was apparently deliberately created to have no relation to anything else.

Wortbildung is the German word meaning '**word-formation**'. However, when used in contrast with *Wortgebildetheit*, it stresses the processual side of the creation of lexemes.

Wortgebildetheit 'word-formedness' provides a contrast with *Wortbildung*. *Wortgebildetheit* looks at the structure of lexemes as they appear in the **lexicon**, rather than the processes by which they were created. The two may not match, for example in instances of **back-formation** and **conversion**. The verb *baby-sit* in English appears to be a compound made up of a noun and a verb. It was, we know, actually created by back-formation from *baby-sitting* and *baby-sitter*. If we study *baby-sit* from the point of view of *Wortbildung*, we see that it is an instance of back-formation, while from the point of view of *Wortgebildetheit* it is a compound verb.

WP see **word-and-paradigm**

wug is an invented word used in a classic experiment by Jean Berko Gleason. Gleason presented her child subjects with a drawing of a bird-like looking creature and said 'This is a wug.' She then produced a new drawing of two of the creatures side by side, and said 'Now there are two of them, there are two —'. The subjects filled in the appropriate form, thereby demonstrating that they could generate plural forms for words they had never heard before, and so had not memorised all the plural forms they used. The experiment has been refined by later scholars, but the original insight has not been affected. Some morphology has to be produced during the act of speaking rather than learnt from exposure to correct models.

Z

zero-derivation see **conversion**

zero morph or **zero morpheme** The genitive plural of a feminine noun in Russian has the form of a bare stem. No other form in the paradigm is without a suffix. Rather than say there is no suffix here, some scholars prefer to say there is a suffix but it has zero form. Thus the genitive plural of *kniga* 'book' is written *knig·Ø*. Strictly, a zero morph is an oxymoron, since a morph is a form and a zero is an absence of form. Zero morphs, sometimes called 'zero morphemes', are always controversial, and a proliferation of zeroes is usually a sign of a poor analysis. In any case, a distinction should be drawn between a zero morph and the lack of any morph because a particular category or property is **unmarked**.

Fundamental Works

These are some fundamental works in morphology (even if they are not books that deal exclusively with morphology). Where a reference is made in the text by name alone, the reference is to the works in this section.

Anderson, Stephen R. (1992). *A-Morphous Morphology*. Cambridge: Cambridge University Press.

Aronoff, Mark (1976). *Word Formation in Generative Grammar*. Cambridge, MA: MIT Press.

Bauer, Laurie (2003 [1988]). *Introducing Linguistic Morphology* (2nd edn). Edinburgh: Edinburgh University Press.

Bloomfield, Leonard (1935 [1933]). *Language*. London: Allen and Unwin.

Bybee, Joan (1985). *Morphology*. Amsterdam and Philadelphia: Benjamins.

Harris, Zellig S. (1951). *[Methods in] Structural Linguistics*. Chicago and London: University of Chicago Press.

Hockett, Charles F. (1958). *A Course in Modern Linguistics*. New York: Macmillan.

Lyons, John (1968). *Introduction to Theoretical Linguistics*. Cambridge: Cambridge University Press.

Martinet, André (1960). *Éléments de linguistique générale*. Paris: Armand Colin.

Matthews, P. H. (1991 [1974]). *Morphology* (2nd edn). Cambridge: Cambridge University Press.

Nida, Eugene A. (1949). *Morphology: The descriptive analysis of words* (2nd edn). Ann Arbor: University of Michigan Press.

Select Bibliography of Books on Morphology

Suggested books for beginners are marked with a single asterisk (*), while rather more complex works which are still relatively approachable are marked with two asterisks (**). Only books written (largely) in English are listed here. This has the unfortunate result of excluding some excellent discussions of individual languages which have wider implications, but the great advantage of making some kind of reasonable coverage possible. Highly theoretical and narrowly focused works have mostly been omitted from the list, as have most sets of conference proceedings, although this involved making very subjective decisions from time to time. Only books are listed, and the one journal that focuses on morphological matters. Many important insights into morphological structure and theory have been published in articles, but no attempt is made to list those.

Adams, Valerie (1973). *An Introduction to Modern English Word-Formation*. London: Longman.
A thorough taxonomy of word-formation in modern English, which discusses some categories often omitted in earlier studies.

Adams, Valerie (2001). *Complex Words in English*. Harlow: Longman.
A reference work on English compounding and derivation that also considers reanalysis and phonesthemes.

Anderson, Stephen R. (1992). *A-Morphous Morphology*. Cambridge: Cambridge University Press.
An important theoretical book, in which morphology without morphs or morphemes is explored in detail.

Aronoff, Mark (1976). *Word Formation in Generative Grammar*. Cambridge, MA: MIT Press.
This was the first major work bringing morphology into generative grammar, and remains very influential.

Aronoff, Mark (1994). *Morphology by Itself*. Cambridge, MA: MIT Press.
A theoretical argument for the independence of morphology from

phonology and syntax. This work introduces the morphome.

*Bauer, Laurie (1983). *English Word-formation*. Cambridge: Cambridge University Press.

This is now theoretically old-fashioned, but raises important questions for the study of word-formation in English.

Bauer, Laurie (2001). *Morphological Productivity*. Cambridge: Cambridge University Press.

A detailed consideration of productivity in general, but with a particular coverage of English morphology.

*Bauer, Laurie (2003). *Introducing Linguistic Morphology* (2nd edn). Edinburgh: Edinburgh University Press.

A wide-ranging textbook, which considers some schools of morphological study as well as some problems of morphology.

Beard, Robert (1995). *Lexeme-Morpheme Base Morphology*. Albany, NY: State University of New York Press.

A presentation of Beard's theory of morphology.

Beard, Robert and Bogdan Szymanek (1988). *Bibliography of Morphology, 1960–1985*. Amsterdam and Philadelphia: Benjamins.

An important bibliographic source.

Blake, Barry J. (2001). *Case* (2nd edn). Cambridge: Cambridge University Press.

A full discussion of case and case systems.

Booij, Geert E. (2001). *The Morphology of Dutch*. Oxford: Oxford University Press.

Although dealing with the morphology of Dutch, this book can also be read as an introduction to morphological thought through the medium of Dutch examples.

Booij, Geert and Jaap van Marle (eds) (1988–). *Yearbook of Morphology*. Dordrecht: Kluwer. [1988–1990 published by Foris]

This is the only periodical devoted to morphological studies. Much of the content is highly technical, but it shows where the latest work in morphology is being done and what the current problems are seen as being.

Booij, Geert, Christian Lehmann, Joachim Mugdan (eds) (2000). *Morphologie: Ein internationales Handbuch zur Flexion und Wortbildung/Morphology: An international handbook on inflection and word-formation*, vol. 1. Berlin and New York: de Gruyter.

Volume one of a proposed two-volume set dealing with all aspects of morphology in a series of commissioned articles. Extremely detailed and authoritative, but sometimes surprisingly readable, too.

**Bybee, Joan L. (1985). *Morphology*. Amsterdam and Philadelphia: Benjamins.

A typological approach to morphology, which considers in particular the order of morphs in verbs across a number of languages.

**Carstairs-McCarthy, Andrew (1992). *Current Morphology*. London and New York: Routledge.

A textbook on morphology which deals with the problems of morphology rather than the schools of morphology. Not aimed at the beginner, but frequently useful for its insights despite this.

*Carstairs-McCarthy, Andrew (2002). *An Introduction to English Morphology*. Edinburgh: Edinburgh University Press.

A well-presented introduction to the morphology of English and the problems that it poses.

Clark, Eve V. (1993). *The Lexicon in Acquisition*. Cambridge: Cambridge University Press.

A discussion of the way in which children acquire morphologically complex words.

*Coates, Richard (1999). *Word Structure*. London and New York: Routledge.

A particularly well-formulated short introduction to morphology for absolute beginners.

Comrie, Bernard (1976). *Aspect: an introduction to the study of verbal aspect and related problems*. Cambridge: Cambridge University Press.

An introduction to the notion of aspect and the ways that the world's languages use it.

Comrie, Bernard (1985). *Tense*. Cambridge: Cambridge University Press.

An introduction to the notion of tense and the ways that the world's languages use it.

Corbett, Greville G. (1991). *Gender*. Cambridge: Cambridge University Press.

An introduction to the notion of gender and the ways that the world's languages use it.

Corbett, Greville G. (2000). *Number*. Cambridge: Cambridge University Press.

An introduction to the notion of number and the ways that the world's languages use it.

Dahl, Östen (1985). *Tense and Aspect Systems*. Oxford and New York: Blackwell.

An introduction to the notions of tense and aspect and the ways that the world's languages use them.

Di Sciullo, Anna-Maria and Edwin Williams (1987). *On the Definition of Word*. Cambridge, MA: MIT Press.

This book makes clear the distinction between being a lexeme and being listed in the lexicon, and also discusses headedness.

Dixon, R. M. W. and Alexandra Y. Aikhenvald (eds) (2002). *Word: a cross-linguistic typology*. Cambridge: Cambridge University Press.
Although much of this collection is technical, the introductory essay by the editors provides an excellent overview of the notion of word.

Dressler, Wolfgang U. (ed.) (1987). *Leitmotifs in Natural Morphology*. Amsterdam and Philadelphia: Benjamins.
A collection of five papers which between them introduce the theory of Natural Morphology.

Dressler, Wolfgang U. and Lavinia Merlini Barbaresi (1994). *Morpho-pragmatics: diminutives and intensifiers in Italian, German, and other languages*. Berlin and New York: de Gruyter.
A view of morphological structure from a different angle, looking at the motivation behind the morphology.

Hall, Christopher J. (1991). *Morphology and Mind: towards a unified approach to explanation in linguistics*. New York: Routledge.
A psycholinguistic approach to the suffixing preference.

Hammond, Michael and Michael Noonan (1988). *Theoretical Morphology*. San Diego: Academic Press.
A set of conference proceedings with some additional invited papers, to show the range of theoretical morphology at the period.

*Haspelmath, Martin (2002). *Understanding Morphology*. London: Arnold.
A good, modern textbook containing many interesting insights.

Jensen, John T. (1990). *Word Structure in Generative Grammar*. Amsterdam and Philadelphia: Benjamins.
A theoretically rather narrow introduction to morphology, clearly designed as course material for a very specific course. Beware of typographical errors.

*Katamba, Francis (1993). *Morphology*. Basingstoke: Macmillan.
A popular and comprehensible introduction to morphology, despite being quite narrowly focused. Beware minor typographical errors.

*Katamba, Francis (1994). *English Words*. London and New York: Routledge.
In some ways an easier version of Katamba (1993), but with an English focus, and a focus on readers who are not linguistics students.

Katamba, Francis (ed.) (2003). *Morphology*. London: Routledge.
A six-volume set, reproducing the leading articles dealing with morphology.

Lockwood, David G. (1993). *Morphological Analysis and Description*. Tokyo: International Language Sciences.
A slightly idiosyncratic approach to morphology, rejecting generative approaches to morphology and sticking to structuralist ideas within

a new formalism. A lot of useful data.

Lieber, Rochelle (1992). *Deconstructing Morphology*. Chicago and London: Chicago University Press.

A highly theoretical work in which morphology is seen as being subject to the same principles as syntax. Although this is difficult and controversial work, it is a good example of the way in which syntax and morphology can be approached in tandem.

Marchand, Hans (1969). *The Categories and Types of Present-Day English Word-Formation* (2nd edn). Munich: Beck.

The definitive work on English word-formation, a structuralist analysis based on a close analysis of the words in the first edition of *The Oxford English Dictionary*.

Matthews, P. H. (1972). *Inflectional Morphology*. Cambridge: Cambridge University Press.

A discussion of the morphology of the Latin verb within the framework of word-and-paradigm morphology. This was the work that made word-and-paradigm into a serious model for the twentieth century after it had been ignored as simply a part of traditional grammar.

Matthews, P. H. (1991). *Morphology* (2nd edn). Cambridge: Cambridge University Press.

This is not an easy book for beginning students, but it is immensely thoughtful and explores carefully the problems of morphology.

Nida, Eugene A. (1949). *Morphology*. Ann Arbor: University of Michigan Press.

The classic structuralist work on morphology, now mostly useful as a historical document and for the data it presents.

**Pinker, Steven (1999). *Words and Rules*. London: Weidenfeld and Nicolson.

An extremely readable and enjoyable introduction to problems of word-structure from a psychologist's point of view, including the dual-route approach to morphology.

Plag, Ingo (1999). *Morphological Productivity*. Berlin and New York: Mouton de Gruyter.

Deals specifically with choice between affixes for English verbs, based on the data in *The Oxford English Dictionary*, and using an Optimality Theoretic framework.

Scalise, Sergio (1984). *Generative Morphology*. Dordrecht: Foris.

An early textbook on morphology within the generative framework, presenting the theoretical developments of the period clearly. Beware of minor typographical errors.

Selkirk, Elisabeth O. (1982). *The Syntax of Words*. Cambridge, MA: MIT Press.

The original development of the syntax of words approach to morphology.

Siegel, Dorothy (1979). *Topics in English Morphology*. New York: Garland.

The published version of the thesis which introduced level-ordering. This is now theoretically out-dated, but it is still worth reading.

Spencer, Andrew (1991). *Morphological Theory*. Oxford and Cambridge, MA: Blackwell.

The most thorough and most theoretically aware textbook in morphology within the generative paradigm; not for beginners, but useful for seeing how the arguments developed.

**Spencer, Andrew and Arnold M. Zwicky (eds) (1998). *The Handbook of Morphology*. Cambridge and Malden, MA: Blackwell.

A set of commissioned articles covering all of morphology, including some morphological sketches of individual languages. A very thorough coverage of the whole field.

Stein, Gabriele (1973). *English Word-Formation over Two Centuries*. Tübingen: Narr.

A useful bibliography of works on English word-formation.

Štekauer, Pavol (2000). *English Word-Formation*. Tübingen: Narr.

A survey of the work of the main scholars of English word-formation from 1960 to 1995, viewed in the light of Štekauer's own theory.

Štekauer, Pavol and Bogdan Szymanek (2002). *A Bibliography of English Word-Formation (1960–2000)*. Presov: Filozofická Fakulta Presovskej Univerzity.

An update on Stein (1973).

Indexes

Each name and language in these indexes is listed alongside the name of the article where a reference is made.